THEY HAVE THEIR EXITS

They Have Their Exits

Airey Neave

With a Foreword by Lord Justice Birkett

CORONET BOOKS
Hodder Paperbacks Ltd., London

First published 1953 by Hodder & Stoughton Ltd
Coronet edition 1970
Second impression 1972

Printed and bound in Great Britain for
Coronet Books,
Hodder Paperbacks Ltd,
St. Paul's House, Warwick Lane,
London, EC4P 4AH
by Hazell Watson & Viney Ltd,
Aylesbury, Bucks

ISBN 0 340 10524 0

To
Diana, Marigold,
and Patrick Neave

MAPS AND DIAGRAMS

FOREWORD

Mr. AIREY NEAVE, the author of this book, is known to a considerable number of people as a rising young barrister and politician. In these two honourable but hazardous professions, the eager aspirant for distinction must be content for a time to be known by the few rather than the many. But Mr. Neave, having a great story to tell, has now written a most moving and fascinating account of a memorable chapter in his life under the title of *They Have Their Exits*; and it is to me a particular pleasure to commend the author and his work to the attention of the wider reading public. The title was no doubt difficult to resist. It has a singular aptness about it, with an underlying touch of humour that is most fully appreciated when the book has been read. But this tense and exciting narrative is not concerned with the entrances and exits of men and women on to the world's stage to play their familiar parts. The only exits here described are those that lead the brave and high-spirited prisoner of war from the shackles of captivity to his former world of action and opportunity. Many others have already written on the same theme, and at this distance of time from the great events, the world has been made well aware of the daring and resource of men and women in the bright face of danger. But none of those who have written of what befell them have had the unique experience that the whirligig of time brought to Mr. Neave, and which he has used in this book with such dramatic effect. The young lieutenant of 1940, wounded, captured, imprisoned, suffering intense humiliation, yet lived to be the Major of 1945, who was appointed by the judges at the International Military Tribunal at Nuremberg to a position that brought him into the closest touch with the Nazi leaders when they were, in turn, captured and imprisoned on the collapse of the German Reich. It is this vivid contrast of the escaped prisoner of war set in authority over KEITEL, GOERING, HESS, RIBBENTROP, FRANK and the rest, that gives to this book a quality that no other book of the like kind possesses.

Mr. Neave was taken prisoner by the Germans at Calais

in 1940. He made two unsuccessful attempts to escape, but from the supposedly impregnable fortress of COLDITZ, to which he had been moved to discourage all further attempts, he made his successful exit with another brave companion; and together they made their perilous way through Switzerland, France and Spain to England. These prosaic sentences convey little in themselves, but to those with eyes to see and ears to hear, they speak of all that this book contains: the high resolve of courageous men to break their bonds; the moments of weariness and loneliness; the suspense and danger and sickening fear; the cold and hunger and thirst and utter wretchedness; and the hope that never died, because it was sustained and nourished by a candle that could never be put out.

When I first met Mr. Neave I was one of the British judges at Nuremberg in 1945. I knew nothing then of his background of Eton, Oxford and the Temple, or of the tremendous experiences of this book. I knew him as a soldier to whom the judges confided the supremely important work of which he speaks in these pages. He discharged that task with ability, tact and unwearied patience, and I welcome the opportunity of paying my tribute to him. His work was the more commendable when it is remembered that he took into the cells at Nuremberg the recollection of all that he had himself endured at the hands of those to whom he now ministered.

"As I looked at Keitel, this strange reversal of fortune brought other memories. I had heard of Mike Sinclair shot down as he tried to escape from the castle at Colditz, of the murders at Stalag Luft III, and the gallant gentlemen in green berets shot without trial. It was this man sitting before me who had carried out these brutal orders ... no crocodile tears for Keitel."

Naturally, there is a note of exultation that the mighty have been put down from their seats, but there is also the note of satisfaction that justice has overtaken evil men, and the grim reflection that though the mills of God may grind slowly, they nevertheless grind exceeding small.

This book then is a story of the most enthralling kind, with here and there touches of humour and even gaiety, here and there the deeper tones of tragedy and loss, and throughout a revelation of the essential nobility of men and women, when faced with the most desperate and dreadful circumstances. For Mr. Neave has written more than his own story. No man escapes without helpers. No man, having escaped, reaches safety without the loyalty and devotion of obscure men and women, who take their lives in their hands when they aid him. And the final impression of the book, therefore, is of the unconquerable spirit of man displayed in many countries and by many people, of the deathless loyalty of men and women to each other in the extremes of peril and adversity, and of the true valour that in some measure redeems the waste, the tragedy and the irreparable loss.

I certainly hope that this book will be widely read.

NORMAN BIRKETT

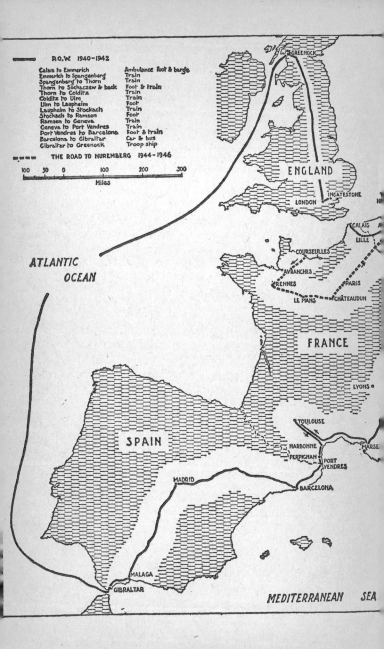

P.O.W. 1940-1942

Calais to Emmerich	Ambulance, foot & barge
Emmerich to Spangenberg	Train
Spangenberg to Thorn	Train
Thorn to Sochaczew & back	Foot & train
Colditz to Ulm	Train
Ulm to Laupheim	Foot
Laupheim to Stockach	Train
Stockach to Ramsen	Foot
Ramsen to Geneva	Train
Geneva to Port Vendres	Foot & train
Port Vendres to Barcelona	Train
Barcelona to Gibraltar	Car & bus
Gibraltar to Greenock	Troop ship

THE ROAD TO NUREMBERG 1944-1946

100 50 0   100   200   300

Miles

ATLANTIC

OCEAN

ENGLAND

GREENOCK

INGATESTONE

LONDON

HA

CALAIS

LILLE

COURSEULLES

AVRANCHES

PARIS

RENNES

LE MANS

CHÂTEAUDUN

FRANCE

LYONS

SPAIN

TOULOUSE

NARBONNE

MARSE

PERPIGNAN

PORT
VENDRES

MADRID

BARCELONA

MALAGA

GIBRALTAR

MEDITERRANEAN   SEA

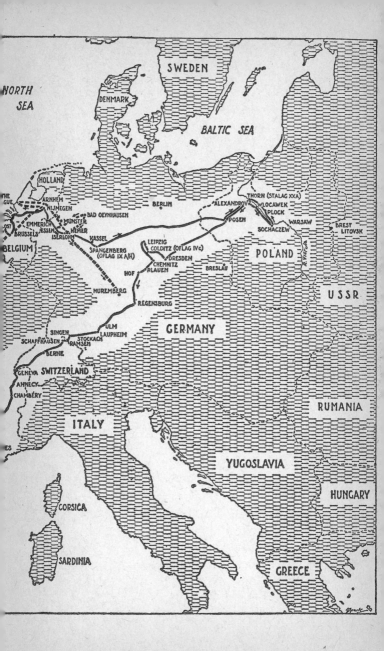

AUTHOR'S NOTE

My thanks are due to Miss Dormer Creston, Mr. Charles Sutton and Major P. R. Reid, M.B.E., M.C., for their help in reading the proofs and making many admirable suggestions.

For reasons of security I have altered the pseudonyms of my French Résistance helpers in Chapters 9, 10 and 11.

CHAPTER I

THE man I had come so far to meet was waiting for me. He stood with his back to the window of his cell in the autumn sunlight. He was tall and grey and with tired eyes he watched our little group as it entered the cell. It seemed that his mouth quivered as he waited at attention until Colonel Andrus, the Governor of the Nuremberg Prison, had taken his place beside the bed.

"Wilhelm Keitel?" I said.

"Yes."

"I am Major Neave, the officer appointed by the International Military Tribunal to serve upon you a copy of the Indictment in which you are named as Defendant."

From somewhere in the prison came the clink of keys. A door was slammed with sudden fierceness. The General Secretary of the Tribunal, the American Prison Chaplain, the Psychiatrist and a group of white-helmeted military policemen crowded the entrance to the cell. They waited eagerly to play their part in the making of History.

I watched the man gather his courage. His square head was held high and he stood there immovable and military, yet utterly woebegone. It was the hour of retribution for General-Fieldmarshal Keitel, Chief of the High Command of the German Armed Forces, member of the Secret Cabinet Council, member of the Council of Ministers for the Defence of the Reich.

Standing before him I was reminded of the words of his countryman, von Logau, describing the slow grinding of the mills of God. It was my duty to set in motion the great proceedings which were to end in his execution as a common murderer.

His field-grey tunic was shorn of decorations and badges of rank and he wore a General Officer's grey breeches with a red stripe. Then suddenly I saw his feet. They were swathed in felt slippers many sizes too large. I wanted to laugh my head off. But at least he was not forced, as I had been, to wear clogs or stand with his feet bare on the stone floor of a Gestapo prison. In spite of his ridiculous appearance, he wore a better uniform than the one in which I tried to escape from a German prisoner of war camp. I could not suppose that Keitel would remember the incident. I was only a Lieutenant in the Royal Artillery aged 24, one of the thousands who lingered in the prisoner of war camps under his command. He had never heard of me or known that I was hungry, cold and friendless and of no account. Yet I had often seen his hard features in German newspapers and wondered about the all-powerful Keitel in those hopeless days. He was a man I had long wanted to meet. I had never thought that I should see him as *my* prisoner and be an official of the Court which tried him for his crimes.

Keitel did remember. In the last days of October 1945, when the Nuremberg defendants were awaiting their trial, I used to interview them in a room in the Palace of Justice. It was my task to arrange for them to be represented by German lawyers. One morning American guards brought Keitel to me to discuss his choice of counsel. I sat at a table and bade him take a chair in front of me. There was no one with us save the guard and an interpreter as my thoughts returned to that counterfeit German uniform which I had devised with such care and patience but which had suffered such an ignominious end. It was coloured with scenery paint from the camp theatre which, while of an authentic field-grey in the dim light of my prison quarters, shone a bright emerald green under the arc lamps outside. I looked more like a demon in a pantomime than an escaping prisoner. The sentries laughed when they caught me and led me off to the cells. I told the sad Field-Marshal of my theatrical attempt to escape from the camp at Colditz in Saxony. He smiled a little and studied my new service dress and Sam Browne.

"Ach so!" he said. "Yes. I remember that camp. Your comrades in Colditz were a trouble to us."

I did not smile. As I looked at Keitel, this strange reversal of fortune brought other memories. I had heard of Mike Sinclair shot down as he tried to escape from the Castle of Colditz, of the murders at Stalag Luft III, and gallant gentlemen in green berets shot without trial. It was this man sitting before me who had carried out those brutal orders. Keitel, the toady to Hitler, the time-serving Staff Officer,

14

the square-headed murderer. No crocodile tears for Keitel. The interview was over.

The discussion which I had with Keitel about his choice of counsel occurred some days after I gave him his copy of the indictment. On that October afternoon in 1945 when I first entered his cell my thoughts were of my own escapes. I looked at the bare white walls, the barred window high above Keitel's head and I felt again that urge to break out. It had always been with me since my two unsuccessful and one successful attempts in twenty months of imprisonment to escape from Germany. When the door slams and the keys are quiet there is time for reflection on infinite possibilities of success. The simplest object in the cell takes on the significance of life and death. The fragment of wire, the nail painfully extracted from the wooden frame of the bed, the smallest morsel of glass or metal, all can become instruments of precision, studded with diamonds, in the hands of the escaper. The escaper is a man who must never admit defeat. He is always ready to attempt the unknown and to achieve the impossible with the minimum of aid.

Keitel never tried to escape from Nuremberg, for escape is not only a technique but a philosophy. The real escaper is more than a man equipped with compass, maps, papers, disguise and a plan. He has an inner confidence, a serenity of spirit which make him a Pilgrim. For Keitel there was no Promised Land to seek.

Colonel Andrus grunted impatiently, and now I saw that once more Keitel's lips were quivering. He has had his day, I thought, this broken martinet. He has only his memories. A Field-Marshal's baton from the Fuehrer; victory in the West and Deutschland Über Alles at the Potsdamer Bahnhof; all the pomp and glory of Prussian militarism in the service of a maniac. I had my memories too, though Keitel was old enough to be my father. I remembered the big grey tourer that brought Goering to Calais in the summer of 1940, passing the British wounded in a cloud of dust. The little German under-officer at the Transit Camp at Alost in Belgium, crimson with anger and wounded pride, shouting at captured British officers as they laughed defiantly at the mildew covering their ration of coarse brown bread.

"Stop laughing, English gentlemen!" Hands on hips, he roared in emulation of the Fuehrer.

"We have no colonies!"

All the tragedy of German inferiority was in that parrot-cry. That night the British officers were made to sleep on stone floors and wait for their bread until coloured soldiers from the French Colonial Army were served.

The wheel had turned a full circle. Could I forget the Jew pushed from the pavement by the S.S. men, his hat spinning in the wind? Or the silence of great dark Polish forests as I crouched among the pine trees in the bitter night? Or the moment when the sentry turned his back before I crossed the frontier into Switzerland at the end of my third escape? Or in later years, the old Frenchwoman who refused to betray hidden British pilots to the Gestapo? Or the Dutch Resistance with whom I worked so long after the Battle of Arnhem?

Defeat had come to the scarecrow remains of Hitler's 1,000-year Reich. Generals, admirals and politicians, they waited for me that autumn day. Perhaps there was on Keitel's lips the well-worn cry of the defeated German.

"We are all soldiers!"

We were not the same sort of soldiers, Keitel and I. Keitel had taken the soldier's oath of allegiance to his Imperial warlord the Kaiser and to Corporal Hitler. I had received a registered envelope from the War Office in 1935 containing a parchment which informed me that His Majesty, King George V, sent greetings to his trusted and well-beloved

Airey Neave

and appointed him to a commission as Second Lieutenant in his Territorial Army.

Keitel began his training in some Prussian military school amid the rigid discipline and efficiency of the Kaiser's Army. I began mine among the Wiltshire Downs at an annual camp with an Infantry Battalion. The sun beat down upon my Platoon as we hid from the enemy behind the chalk hills and listened expectantly for the sound of blank cartridges. I lay on my back beside a wooden Lewis gun. God was in his heaven and the crickets chatted merrily in the dry grass. A Small Copper, a Fritillary and even a Clouded Yellow flew past me. Nearby the men were laughing happily, clustered around the lip of a chalk pit. We were not prepared for war. We never are.

Out of that blue sky an enemy appeared, with a red and black armband designed to inspire terror. Then came another, and finally, more awful than all, a real live Brigadier. He had a sour, yellowish face. He was dressed as if for manoeuvres before the First World War, with leggings and a panoply of leather cases and belts and straps. He glared in my direction as I began to rise gingerly from the turf. My ridiculous plus-fours and puttees, the only nether garments the War Office could design for infantry subalterns, were covered in chalk and bits of grass.

"Lie down there!" shouted the Brigadier.

I could see his glasses glinting angrily in the sun. In a few minutes the last blank was fired, the flags representing Hitler's forces were pulled up and little groups began to converge upon the chalk-pit to discuss the battle. The officers stood in a circle looking apprehensive. I could see the Brigadier and the Colonel looking in my direction. The Brigadier's glasses flashed menacingly, and the other subalterns began to take pity on me. My plight gave them courage as they exclaimed eagerly,

"What has Neave been doing?"

There is a maxim in the law that he who voluntarily submits himself to the risk of serious injury is not to recover damages. It seemed to me that my Territorial service was entirely governed by this principle. Why had I condemned myself to be tortured by this Brigadier? He began to speak, working himself slowly into a cold, terrifying anger at the conduct of my platoon. A position had been chosen that could be seen for miles around. He had seen the men in the chalk-pit with his own eyes from his imaginary headquarters. Soon his oratory took on the style of Sergeant Buzfuz. He declared that he had never seen such ridiculous positions. As for my platoon-sergeant in the chalk-pit, his left flank was entirely unprotected. Why had not—

I rose to my feet.

"There was an imaginary platoon on his left flank, Sir, I posted it there."

Even on Salisbury Plain you could have heard a pin drop. My Colonel, white in the face, stared at the ground. The Brigadier gulped.

"Now perhaps I may continue with what I had to say."

But the spell was broken. Congratulations rained on me

in the Mess and the old songs were sung far into the night. This was the manner of my preparation for the gathering storm when I was nineteen.

In those days Joachim von Ribbentrop called the British decadent. His foreign policy, conducted on this assumption, earned him the title from Hitler of the second Bismarck. According to his standards my upbringing unfitted me for any form of manly conflict whatever. I had, in the first place been educated at Eton. Eton was an institution which exercised a strong fascination for Nazi philosophers. I remember the enormous significance that an S.S. interrogator attached to this revelation when he was asking me how I had succeeded in escaping from a prison-camp in Poland. Eton to him was not merely decadent and snobbish, it was mysterious, sinister and incalculable. In Nazi teaching, Old Etonians were soft but cunning and should therefore be carefully watched and reports compiled about their activities. Their conversation was regarded as unintelligible and possibly conducted in code. They spoke in a dialect of their own, known as the Oxford accent. The wearing of top hats by young aristocrats was of more than social or class importance. It indicated something deeper, possibly connected with the science of astrology. Had not Heinrich Himmler himself ordered a department of the Reich Security Main Office to conduct research into the wearing of this headgear by Eton boys?

I looked again at Keitel's blank, miserable Prussian face and thought of the year 1934, when it was fashionable in some quarters to declare that no one but a very stupid undergraduate would fight for his King and Country. This was an Oxford where a few brave spirits still tried to emulate the joyful irresponsibility of the 'twenties. In the 'thirties the shadows lengthened and the voice of Adolf Hitler threatened across the waters but it had little effect upon my undergraduate world. To be a Territorial was distinctly eccentric. Military service was a sort of archaic sport as ineffective as a game of croquet on a vicarage lawn and far more tiresome. "Playing at soldiers": I have heard that phrase so often, and yet within a few short years the decadents, the fantastics and the intellectuals were fighting for their very lives.

Von Ribbentrop, who occupied a cell near Keitel, was too

shaken by a fate that put him under lock and key at the hands of the degenerate Anglo-Saxon "business men," to discuss with me his former theories. And yet my Oxford career would have served as a good illustration of his basic assumptions. I did little academic work for three years and then was obliged to work feverishly at the law in order to get a degree. I made three speeches at the Oxford Union, in one of which I found myself discussing the motion of the week before. My failure to understand the merits of the fashionable intellectual notions of Socialism was regarded as a sign of mental deficiency by the dons. The climax of my "Oxford education" was a champagne party on top of my College tower when empty bottles came raining down to the grave peril of those below. The College showed great forbearance and even kindliness throughout this dismal performance. I shall always be grateful to them. From Oxford, I went to London to read for the Bar. Few cared about Hitler and even less about his ambassador, Ribbentrop. Debutantes "came out" and went their way. It was fashionable to be almost inarticulate on any serious subject.

When the war broke out I was no longer an infantryman and my tasks in the Territorial Army were unromantic. The operation of searchlights, however bright, is not, in my opinion, a shining form of warfare. It did not conform to my desire to be in the field with Rupert Brooke and other heroes of the past. It so happened that after six months in a muddy field in Essex, I was posted to a searchlight training regiment at Hereford. I had now become a "gunner," a very comprehensive term in the British Army. From Hereford I crossed to Boulogne in February 1940, in charge of an advance party of rugged old veterans of the first war. In France, the searchlights were treated by everyone with meagre respect. An officer of the Guards described them to me as "quite Christmassy." I kept my counsel and waited for the underdogs to show their mettle.

The dark green helmet of Colonel Andrus, as he stood in Keitel's cell in 1945, reflected a pin-point of sun beside the coat of arms emblazoned on its face. This coat of arms, designed by the worthy Prison Governor and his staff, comprised a key ending in a broken swastika with scales of Justice above a shattered German eagle in heraldic flames. These symbolic flames seemed a little inappropriate. Had I not seen the great black cloud of smoke which darkened the horizon over Dunkirk billowed out across the Channel? I had come with my battery from Arras to Calais to take part in the last stand before Dunkirk. Along the straight roads past Vimy Ridge and St. Omer to a village outside Calais called Coulogne, the straggling columns of refugees choked every road. Led by their priests, they wandered like a forlorn crusade. Spies and deserters, refugees from Hitler, filled the little village square to an accompaniment of shrieks from the dying. And we, voluntary soldiers and conscripts of His Majesty, ready to die, or at any rate expecting to die, stood amid this turmoil with two anti-tank rifles to meet the might of Rommel's panzers. Hopefully, we dragged tables and chairs from the school, placed the village hearse across the road and waited.

I sat under the chestnut tree in front of the Mairie on that hot afternoon of May 23rd, 1940. Was it possible for human beings to have created such nightmare disorder, or was this a glimpse of the real hell? Then I thought of my expensive education and laughed, and as I dozed, I saw a room in the Temple where I had been a pupil in the Chambers of an eminent barrister, and a volume lay open at the title "The Fatal Accidents Act."

The mortar bomb was nearly fatal. It burst on the roof of the Mairie and showered tiles and pieces of chestnut at my feet. Several followed, bursting with great accuracy among the refugees. Beside each wall, were little huddled groups sheltering from the fire and above, in a clear blue sky, droned a Fieseler Storch light aeroplane as happy as a lark. I fired at it wildly with a rifle, but it flew away like a victorious partridge and disappeared behind a captured hospital train where the mortars were busy. Beside me on the pavement lay the dead body of my despatch rider, thrown from his machine to the other side of the road. I took his papers and looked down at him. He had been a cheerful man. He still had a smile that even a mortar bomb could not efface.

Towards evening we were ordered to retire from the village. The narrow streets were hung with broken telegraph wires. And, as we hurried into Calais, only the church spire could be seen above the smoke which covered our retreat. The Rifle Brigade, the 60th Rifles, and the Queen Victoria's

Rifles had begun to land and in the same moment that they set foot in France the enemy began to shell the docks. Hasty defences were improvised. The new arrivals were full of information. They assured me that the enemy consisted entirely of motor cyclists. A Major glared at me like the Brigadier of that far-off summer day, when I told him that these motor-cyclists had blown the village of Coulogne to bits. We were ordered to await the enemy in the sand dunes on the west side of the town. Over my head the shells screamed and as Calais became still and dark they burst with a staccato crash in the docks behind us. And then out of that heavy silence came the sound of a guitar. A baby cried. . . .

The attack began in earnest next morning, hesitatingly at first, and then, towards the afternoon of the 24th May, tanks began to break through. I was sent to the east side of the town, the hot pavement burned the soles of my feet and the rifle I carried had become more of an encumbrance than a weapon. The men, inexperienced, some frightened, others weary and hoping for evacuation, were led to the Boulevard Gambetta. Bullets struck the pavement and bounced off the walls with a noise like the crack of a whip. Here and there a white face showed at a cellar grating. A macabre group appeared dodging the fire and carrying the corpse of an old woman across the boulevard. And in the heat of that afternoon, as Keitel was telephoning his Fuehrer's orders to the west from the comfort of Berlin, an old Crusader tank fired a round or two up the boulevard. As it gingerly withdrew, I felt a sharp blow in my side. I crawled a few yards. I felt the blood running down inside my clothes and trickle to my stomach.

"Are you all right, Sir?" said a hoarse voice.

"Get me some Cognac quick—from the café."

I got to my feet and leant against the wall. A bespectacled medical orderly came up to me as if from nowhere. He squinted at the wound and grinned maddeningly.

"You're a lucky one, Sir. 'Arf an inch from the 'eart. Only a flesh wound."

Bandaged and faint I came to a vast stone hospital near the docks, and all next day the Stukas came and went at will. But there was no surrender. The wounded lay packed together in the darkness of the hospital cellars and, above the bombardment, I heard strange snatches of conversation.

"Une belle amputation."

"The Major of the Rifle Brigade has got up and gone back to his unit."

"Tant mieux."

"Good luck to both of you."

The Corporal and I were able to walk. Perhaps we could still organise the evacuation of those less seriously wounded. We crawled beneath the battered doors of the hospital, which would not open, into the smoke and flame of the town. A hand at the level of the pavement passed out a bottle of wine from a crowded cellar and then, the Corporal vanished in a blinding flash and dust.

It was much too late. On the platforms of the Gare Maritime where a few months before travellers had started gaily for Paris, the last stand was made among the wagons-lits and in the sand dunes. A man shot himself with his own rifle in an archway which housed the regimental aid post; beside me a young soldier was crying quietly. A field-grey figure appeared shouting and waving a revolver. Then a huge man in German uniform and a Red Cross armband put me gently on a stretcher. I was a prisoner of war.

I wondered what were Keitel's feelings when he was taken prisoner? Did he feel, as I felt, that life was over, and the purpose for which one was made was suddenly gone? When I was better I started with a host of others on the march to Germany, through Belgium from one foul transit camp to another until we came to the mouth of the Scheldt. A huge barge awaited us and in its hold, black with coal dust, we lay for three days and nights as we chugged towards the Rhine. It was a voyage of lost souls crossing into the unknown. One hot evening we passed under the Nijmegen bridge. A girl waved to us from the parapet. The light breeze caught her skirt. There was a round of homesick laughter as the barge crawled on into the night. And yet, Keitel, I lived to cross the Nijmegen bridge as a victor just four years afterwards and saw the dead Germans on the sidewalks as we made all speed for Arnhem!

The General Secretary of the Tribunal handed me a list of German lawyers.

I spoke again to Keitel:

"Under Article 16 of the Charter of the Tribunal you may

have counsel of your own choice or the Tribunal may appoint counsel for you."

I handed him the list and a copy of the Charter of the Tribunal. He took the documents and tried to click his heels, but the felt slippers did not respond. I did not return the salute.

"Please read these documents. If you have any questions you may address them to me tomorrow."

I was curt. I was impatient to go. The past was now forgotten. There were other visits to make, each one providing its own drama. The door was shut in Keitel's face as he stood erect and helpless, holding his papers, and next to his cell another door was flung open. A vast figure in dove grey lifted itself from the bed.

"Hermann Goering?" I said.

CHAPTER II

It is August 1940. High above the town of Spangenburg near Kassel stands the castle which is now the prisoner of war camp known as Oflag IXA/H. Its arched doorways and clock tower remind me of school. A school to which, it seems, our fathers have been before us. This castle has been a prisoner of war camp in the past, and we are a new generation of captives. We sleep in the eternal two-tiered beds with the same palliasses and rough blankets. We have our same sad possessions, packed away. Our Red Cross chocolate and carefully hoarded delicacies are guarded like a schoolboy's tuck box. Precious letters full of love and hope, or bitter betrayal, are hidden in some cheap suitcase or kitbag. In those letters is our dream world.

Readers of escape books have grown familiar with the Oflags and the Stalags, and the scenery of barbed wire and sentries. They have heard the jargon of camps, the nicknames for familiar Germans, and the pathetic jokes which illumine the tragedy of the prisoner's life. For such imprisonment is a double tragedy. First, there is the loss of freedom. Then, since there is no apparent crime to expiate, unless it be personal folly, a sense of injustice scars the spirit.

This bitterness of soul has clouded the life of many a strong man.

The prisoner of war is to himself an object of pity. He feels he is forgotten by those who flung him, so he thinks, into an unequal contest. He broods over the causes of his capture, and to himself and his friends he soon becomes a bore, endlessly relating the story of his last stand. In these interminable reminiscences he unites with his fellow-prisoners in a chorus of protest at his sudden removal from active service.

For me the days passed wearily and I have no wish to re-live them. There were strict codes of behaviour designed for us by our senior officers, and social cliques appeared from the very first day. I attempted to write for the camp magazine, but my articles were rapidly dismissed as unsuitable. It is dangerous to tamper with the literary views of the average British officer. Any attempt at being funny in a jelligraph camp magazine is doomed to failure and will very likely lead to ostracism. Not that the criticisms of my fellow-prisoners were unjustified.

From the point of view of architecture, the castle had little to commend it. There was a drawbridge at the entrance with a vaulted gateway where a sentry stood. Grey buildings surrounded a courtyard of the roughest cobblestones, fit only for clogs, with which all prisoners were issued by the Germans. We could walk along a pathway beside the battlements, which overlooked a moat, and watch the sentries on the other side. On clear days there was a narrow view of farm lands and blue-green hills beyond the last defences of the castle.

After an eternity of despair and boredom I was moved with others to a new camp in the village in the woods below the castle. The boundary of this camp adjoined a stream which rushed along beside a muddy roadway, where children laughed and played in freedom. The prisoners, waking each morning to the noise of geese and other rural sounds, fancied themselves part of this unfettered life. It was a kinder atmosphere than that of the gaunt castle, perched remotely on its hill. Here the winter months of 1940 passed in discomfort, but without great suffering, unless it be of the soul. There was little food, and soon the stomach, accustomed to a meagre diet, could not adjust itself to an unusual quantity. A whole tinned steak-and-kidney pudding for each prisoner was saved for Christmas. I could not finish mine.

In February 1941 we were moved by train to Poland, to the vast encampment of Stalag XXa. This measure was described as a reprisal for the alleged ill-treatment of German officers in Canada. In an old Polish fort, surrounded by a moat, at Thorn on the banks of the Vistula, hundreds of officers lived in damp, cold, vault-like rooms. A high mound of turf bleakly surrounded a kind of parade ground, and hid the outside world. Every evening at sunset the small group of British orderlies who were with us stood upon the drawbridge above the moat and sang "Abide with me." This was the only moment of hope and reality in all our dismal day.

From this terrible futility, I determined to free myself. The enforced comradeship of others was, so to speak, a form of imprisonment within the prison walls themselves. But it seemed hopeless to try and escape from this grim fort. Even the small area of the parade ground had an air of death. Here Polish patriots had faced the firing squads, their backs to the mound of turf which encircled the parade ground.

Suddenly, there came the inspiration and the plan. I saw my opportunity and took it. A single wooden building had absorbed my fiercely concentrated thoughts. It was the hut in which a captured British dentist worked. It stood within the perimeter of the main camp for N.C.O's. and soldiers, some four miles from the fort. The hut, consisting of a surgery and waiting-room, and behind it a lavatory with corrugated iron roof, stood close to the red brick Kommandantur of Stalag XXa. On the opposite side of a dividing road was a compound of wooden huts and sentry-boxes, winged by barbed wire, where thousands of British soldiers were herded together. Most of them spent their days in large working-parties making roads and aerodromes or clearing a site for fresh huts in the pine forest around the camp. Beyond this forest lay a desert, scarred with shell holes, used by the Germans for artillery practice, and later as a training ground for desert warfare. To the west of the camp lay the great River Vistula, winding through dull, flat country, and on its far bank could be seen the Eastern spires of ancient Thorn. To the east, beyond the artillery ground were more pine

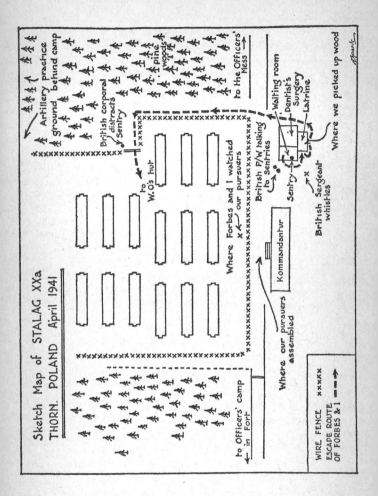

Sketch Map of STALAG XXa THORN. POLAND April 1941

Artillery practice ground behind camp

to pine woods

to the Officers' Mess →

British corporal distracts Sentry

Waiting room
Dentist's Surgery
Latrine

Where we picked up wood

British P/W talking to Sentries

Sentry

British Sergeant whistles

to W.Os' hut

Where Forbas and I watched our pursuers

Kommandantur

Where our pursuers assembled

to Officers' camp in Fort

WIRE FENCE xxxxx
ESCAPE ROUTE OF FORBES & I - - - →

forests and, some twenty miles from the camp, the town of Alexandrov.

A dentist's waiting room is usually associated with the anticipation of painful events. But that bare room with its wooden forms became the focus of all my reasoning and of eager excitement. Fortune favoured me with severely inflamed gums. Their condition, aggravated no doubt by bad food and general weakness, required regular treatment. The Germans, impressed by the need for sound teeth, even in enemy prisoners of war, permitted a number of officers to visit the dentist every Thursday.

They were marched under escort from the fort, to the confines of the main camp at Stalag XXa. For several weeks I marched each Thursday along the tree-lined road, and halted at the dentist's door. On that weekly journey I did not think of my inflamed gums. I dreamed of my triumphant arrival in Russia. It was the spring of 1941, before the Germans attacked Russia, and I believed that, were I to reach the demarcation line held by the Russians at Brest-Litovsk, I should swiftly be ushered into the presence of the British ambassador, Sir Stafford Cripps.

Facts are more important than dreams to the successful escaper. He must leave nothing to chance. For weeks I feverishly recruited allies from the soldiers' camp. Every morning I used to meet a working party as they arrived in the fort to do maintenance jobs. They marched under a British sergeant each day from the main camp, and crossed the drawbridge, after being counted by a German under-officer. They were no more than a dozen in number, but among them were two soldiers from my own battery who had survived the defence of Calais. These men were staunch friends ready to risk a penalty of twenty-eight days solitary confinement for helping an officer to escape. They left each evening, and after a perfunctory search of their clothes at the drawbridge, they marched back to the main camp.

My plan was to escape from the dentist's quarters and conceal myself in the main camp where the men were lodged and in due time to escape from one of the groups of prisoners working in the open. I therefore began to organise my reception in the main camp by sending notes on grubby bits of paper concealed in the clothes of trustworthy friends in the working party as they marched away each evening. One of my keenest helpers was Private Marriott of the 1st Bucks Battn. Oxford and Bucks Light Infantry. Young, fresh-faced and smart, he formed a vital link in the chain of communication. By this furtive correspondence it was arranged that I should hide in the warrant officers' hut.

Then began the transfer of my collection of food for the escape, tin by tin, and packet by packet. By April 1941, the working party had smuggled from the fort a considerable quantity of condensed milk, chocolate and sardines. They took them to the senior warrant officer, a Company Sergeant-Major, who hid them in his hut where I was awaited.

In the three months since our arrival from Spangenburg, several officers had made attempts to escape from the fort without success. Among them three Canadian pilots, Flying Officers Donaldson, Thom and Flynn, in overalls and home-made Luftwaffe forage caps, reached an aerodrome nearby and climbed inside an aircraft to fly to Sweden. They could not start it. Then a harsh voice accosted them from the control tower. Meekly they stood to attention to be admonished for a breach of take-off discipline by an enraged Luftwaffe under-officer who was puzzled by their dumb insolence. Their inability to understand German compelled them to surrender. These three officers had reached the aerodrome by exchanging places with members of the working party which came to the fort from the main camp.

A stricter search of all who entered and left the fort resulted, but my helpers were not deterred. I bought a rough workman's coat and a pair of painter's trousers, poor and ragged, from a British officer who decided to abandon escaping to read for a degree in Law. These clothes travelled to the main camp bundled in the battle-dress of the sergeant in charge of the working party. I now lacked only money, papers and a companion. Money was my least concern. I had a sort of medieval faith that a sack of tinned food and chocolate, which purported to contain the tools of my trade as a Polish carpenter, would suffice me for a journey of two hundred miles to the Soviet lines. I procured a few crumpled Reichsmarks in a black market transaction with a Polish glazier who came to mend some of the fort windows. To him I sold some Players' cigarettes. As for papers, it was impossible to obtain authentic documents for an escaper who intended to pass as a Pole when confronted by Germans, and a German national or Volksdeutsch from Bassarabia when confronted by Poles. I had to find what I could.

John Mansel of the Queen's was a skilful draughtsman who patiently forged papers for escapers throughout a long captivity. In the fort at Thorn he used to sit, hunched at a table in the lamplight, fenced in by crowded two-tiered beds, while fellow-prisoners kept watch for unwelcome Germans. His patient skill produced many passes and identity cards. Someone had procured a green pass for a civilian workman to enter the area of the Kommandantur of Stalag XXa. Mansel supplied copies of this pass for those desiring to escape. The one he made for me described me as a Polish carpenter from Bromberg. I had no documents for the journey into Central Poland.

For many weeks I made my plans unaided but under the direction of the senior British officer, Brigadier the Hon. N. F. Somerset, D.S.O., M.C., and I asked him to find me a companion for the attempt. I wanted someone who could speak good German and who had faith in my scheme. The officers in my room regarded my plans with friendly derision and few could be found who would even discuss them seriously. I had hoped to have as my companion John Hyde-Thomson, M.C., of the D.L.I. He, however, had succeeded in getting out of the camp a few weeks earlier by changing places with C.S.M. Qualtrough. After a long, lone journey across the wastes of western Poland, he was recaptured, and brought back to the fort. The companion to whom I was introduced was Norman Forbes, a Flying Officer in the Royal Air Force, who spoke fluent German. He was a volunteer airman, shot down in 1940 over the French coast, while flying a Hurricane. From the moment we met he shared my plans, and, being both of an original mind, and more practical than myself, we soon were ready to make the attempt.

Norman Forbes was a tall, slender man with fair hair. His features were finely drawn giving an impression of sensitive strength. He had a quick intelligence and an impatience of unnecessary detail. As an escaper he showed great determination and shrewdness. He had been brought up in the religion of Christian Science and had faith in the success of our plan.

Each night before I was due to return to the dentist on the

following Thursday, I lay thinking on my wooden bed. I desired only to be free from the terrible monotony of the fort and once outside under the stars I cared little what happened to me. I dreamed of nights sheltering in the shade of some romantic forest alone in the world. I felt that once outside the camp I should be happy if I were only free for awhile.

I woke on the morning of 16th April, after a refreshing sleep. No anxiety racked or tormented me. I felt with inner conviction that this day meant freedom. I drank my *ersatz* coffee and prepared myself for the march to the dentist's quarters. I joined the officers who required treatment, assembled under an archway at the head of the drawbridge. We stood there talking and from the darkness of the archway there emerged the pale figure of a fellow-prisoner in a tattered French cavalry overcoat. He spoke to me slowly, pressing into my hand a crumpled bit of paper.

"Good luck to both of you," he said quietly. "Please call at this address if you get back and—tell her I love her."

"I will," I said with pride.

There was a guttural shout from a German under-officer, the sentries shouldered their rifles and we marched over the drawbridge. We stopped at the gate where we were counted, and then at a quick pace set off along the road to the main camp. It was a dry, warm day and specks of green were beginning to show over the barren, low-lying countryside. Sad-eyed Polish women passed us on the road, pushing small carts. An aged peasant stood at the doorway of his hovel. Forbes and I were together, he, tall and silent, taking long strides and looking straight before him. Beneath our rough overcoats we wore army battle-dress without badges or marks of rank, and as we marched there was light-hearted talk and banter with the sentries.

"Back home by Christmas!" said a moon-faced German.

"Certainly," I replied, and laughed.

There was good temper everywhere on that fine spring morning. A German staff car, pushing us to the side of the road, carried a General, monocled and threatening in the back seat. Even he did not offend us.

Towards half-past ten, we passed the Kommandantur and came to the dentist's door. In the waiting-room we sat, guarded by one sentry, who stood gazing out of the window with expressionless, slab-like face. Through the window, I could see small groups of British prisoners among the pine trees pushing carts of wood, and from the distance came the strains of "Roll Out the Barrel" as a working party set off into the forest. Outside the door of the waiting-room two guards lounged against the wall of the hut joking with a tall British Sergeant. From time to time the Sergeant glanced nervously towards the corrugated iron roof of the lavatory in the rear of the dentist's surgery. Across the supports beneath the roof he had placed several pieces of wood for us to collect and take into the camp. These were our props for the first scene in the play. The stage was set and the curtain was due to rise.

The dental officer treated my gums. As he applied a brown strong-smelling lotion I blurted out my news to him. He smiled and calmly shook my hand as he summoned the next patient, Norman Forbes, from the waiting-room. Back in the waiting-room there was silence. A light breeze blew among the pines and distant voices shouted in English. The sentry still gazed without expression at the window. Five minutes passed shortening the time to the moment of action. I looked at my watch and at eleven o'clock rose from my chair and pronounced the magic word:

"Abort."

The sentry glanced in my direction with indifference and nodded woodenly. He flung open the door and I stepped into the muddy roadway. The two sentries outside still lounged by the corner of the hut. They did not look my way. There was another actor on the stage who claimed their attention, another ally in the plot to escape. A small, alert British prisoner with long black hair flowing beneath his cap, and side whiskers, was showing them some shining object. His voice was raised in the enthusiasm of his salesmanship. Even at that moment I could see him in felt cap and choker in Petticoat Lane, demonstrating his wares. Swiftly I reached the lavatory, removed my overcoat and placed it in the space beneath the roof where the wood was lying. I gathered up a few pieces of lath and wood and waited for Forbes. He came quickly, bowed his head beneath the rusty roof, placed his overcoat beside mine and took up his share of wood. Another short, tense wait.

The tall British Sergeant was pacing carelessly beside the

lavatory. He whistled softly. At the signal, I walked as naturally as possible behind the hut, and round its far wall out of the view of the sentries. At the roadway I was joined by Forbes and we began to talk and laugh as we walked towards the entrance of the compound on the other side carrying our bits of wood to give the impression that we were employed on some errand. No one shouted. No one even looked in our direction for in the immediate area of the Kommandantur, it was not unusual for prisoners to walk unguarded. The Germans were accustomed to the unquenchable gaiety and genial disobedience of British officers and soldiers. Unlike the captured officers the soldiers were relieved of much of the boredom of prison life by having work to do.

We were now dressed in our battle-dresses without badges of rank, trying to become absorbed in the mass of prisoners. We walked up a lane fenced with posts and wire and reached the main gate. A sentry armed with a bayonet talked casually with a British corporal. He glanced at us unintelligently, and it seemed the corporal gave us a faint wink as we passed through into the haven of the compound. Around us were rows of huts, and orderlies passing busily with brushes and pails. I swung my pieces of wood towards one of the huts out of sight of the main gate. Company Sergeant-Major Thornborough of the Green Howards with clean uniform and shining boots stood at the door. He grinned and shook us both by the hand and we walked with him to the end of the long hut between rows of two-tiered metal beds with blue and white check mattresses.

This was a warrant officers' hut and everything in it shone. The floor and walls were scrubbed and every man's kit and possessions were laid out as if in barracks at home. It seemed to me a homely place. The windows were open and the breeze had the strong scent of pines. I thought of the officers in the fort four miles away, shrouded in the semi-darkness of ammunition chambers, looking through loopholes to the far side of the moat where a *chevaux de frise* of iron spikes was their only horizon. Here, under the command of the genial Sergeant-Major Thornborough all was order and smartness and light.

It was moving to be once more among these staunch friends. The tall sergeant who whistled, the man from Petticoat Lane, and the corporal who occupied the sentry at the main gate, had risked severe punishment to make our plan work. In the hut, beds had been prepared for us and cups of tea were ready at the farthest end from the door, where it was dark. Under the direction of my old Battery Quartermaster-Sergeant Kinnear intricate pains were taken to conceal our presence in the camp. The experience of other attempts had taught us the value of concealment until the search had died down and the hue-and-cry was over. I believed that if we remained for a few days hidden in this hut, the ring of security troops for a radius of twenty-five miles around the camp would be withdrawn and then, after an interval, we could go out with some party working in the woods and escape.

We lay on our beds completely happy at our welcome. Shortly after noon C.S.M. Thornborough came into the hut. He was laughing.

"Come outside and see something good. Take a brush and pail each and pretend to be hut orderlies and mix with the crowd by the wire. If anyone recognises you don't speak to them now. I am afraid we have one or two stool pigeons in the camp."

We followed him across the parade ground trying to look like orderlies being led off to a fatigue, and passing through the line of huts we came to the barbed wire in front of the Kommandantur. Our escape had been discovered an hour before. Around us a crowd of British soldiers were laughing and shouting sallies at the Germans. Opposite, in the roadway, silent but grinning, stood our fellow dental patients. Furious Germans stamped around them. Revolver butts showed from the unbuttoned black holsters of the underofficers, and rifles were held at the ready. Down the steps of the Kommandantur came agitated German officers gesticulating at the crestfallen sentries.

Then came the sound of dogs barking, and along the road a formidable column of S.S. men, armed with tommy guns, marched swiftly towards the camp and halted a few feet from the wire where we stood. Behind them were Field Police leading Alsatian dogs. There was a further shouting of orders and anxious perusal of maps, and the column marched away in the direction of the fort. Fascinated, we watched the departure of our pursuers. The prisoners began

33

to drift away from the wire and we, the quarry of this well-armed band, returned to the warrant officers' hut and lay quietly on our beds.

I slept peacefully in a lower bunk at the end of the hut. Early next morning came an *appel* on the parade ground for the whole of the camp. It was the usual practice for the orderlies detailed to clean out the huts in the early morning to be excused this parade. On this morning all the huts were suddenly cleared. Forbes and I lying on our backs beneath two beds, waited for the sound of footsteps. The hut door was flung open and German voices sounded from somewhere afar off. I lay turned on my side against the wall of the hut, clutching the iron leg of the bed, my cheek against the surface of the wooden floor. The stamping of jackboots on the boards was deafening. Nearer and nearer they came and with them the noise of throaty breathing, so close that it seemed to have reached the level of my ears. My heart beat wildly, for they were looking under the beds. Two rows away from us the stamping of boots stopped. There was grunting, but the footsteps began to die away to the far end of the hut. The door was slammed. Anxiously I craned my head towards the bed where Forbes was hiding.

The Germans suspected that we were in the camp. On that morning they searched every hut and examined the boiler room and other likely hiding places. Why did they suspect? Had we been recognised among those thousands by some informant? I felt that we had taken too great a risk in gazing through the wire at the comedy of the hounds in pursuit of us—the quarry. In the warrant officers' hut there would be no betrayal. All we need do was to hide there and not emerge for several days until the opportunity arose of leaving with a working party at dawn. Every hour our friends brought us news of the search, but the hut was no longer watched.

"I heard from the Jerry in the kitchen that you had been recaptured and mauled by dogs, Sir. Having you here is the biggest laugh we've had on them since we came," said a sergeant from my own battery.

"It will be an even bigger laugh if we get home."

"Best of luck to you, Sir."

These loyal men ran greater risks of punishment than we did, but not one spoke of the consequences. All were anxious only that we, who had the advantage of speaking German, should have the opportunity to get home and give news of their plight. They were short of food and had undergone a terrible winter in which many in the camp had died far from home. Their selflessness touched me deeply.

Three days later we said good-bye and shook hands with everyone in the hut. The C.S.M. saluted discreetly and then shook hands himself. I was sorry to leave these staunch and kindly people. During my stay there had been no feeling of class or rank among us, only a mutual desire to defy the Germans.

At six o'clock on the morning of the 19th April, after a single mug of *ersatz* coffee, a working party of a hundred and fifty men, under C.S.M. Van der Werf assembled near the main gate. Forbes and I, mingling with them, were counted and marched away. It was a dull grey day, and, as we marched, we sang "Roll Out the Barrel" and the "Quartermaster's Stores" until we were beyond the pine forests and halting at a large farm surround by barns and stables. A German warrant officer, roaring at the top of his voice, split the party up into small groups for different tasks among the farm buildings. Our group collected mattress covers which we began to fill with hay and straw from barns and outhouses.

Forbes and I worked under the direction of a British corporal all that morning making palliasses in a great barn. The corporal, when no Germans were watching, whispered directions to us. The barn had doors at either end. One was fastened by a padlock, but the other, least in use, was held in position only by a wooden cross-bar twined with wire. Before the midday meal at noon I saw the corporal loosening the wire so that the door would open easily. I stopped working for a moment on my palliasses to gaze at the hay piled high up to the roof. There was a hoarse voice behind me and I turned. A short red-faced German officer blinked at me through spectacles.

"You there!"

I said nothing and smiled weakly. I caught the corporal's anxious glance. I flung myself at the hay and eagerly began to fill a palliasse. The little officer shook his head and then announced:

"The English must be made to work!"

He remained watching me for a full five minutes. I began to wonder if he recognised me and whether he had been shown my photograph after our escape. Then he turned and walked away muttering to himself about the English who would not work. It was a dangerous moment, and as we entered the farm yard to meet the lorry which brought out the midday ration of coarse brown bread and sausage from the camp, I looked anxiously to see if he was there but he had disappeared.

The ration lorry drew up beside us and I watched it closely. C.S.M. Van der Werf had hidden two men inside. The only German I could see was the driver and then, as it halted, the doors at the back swung open and two khaki figures jumped swiftly down and disappeared in the crowd. It was unnoticed by the guard that the number of the working party had increased to one hundred and fifty-two. It was our plan to hide in the barn when the party marched back to the camp at exactly the same strength as it had left in the morning.

The afternoon dragged on, and as we filled the palliasses I wondered what was happening at the fort. Nearly a week had passed since we escaped from the dentist's hut. Had bloodhounds been used to search for us? We had already hidden every article of clothing that the Germans might find to give the hounds a scent. Friends in our rooms at the fort had exchanged our mattresses after our departure to the dentist. It seemed that the hue and cry was dying down.

Late in the afternoon when no Germans were in the barn, the corporal stood by the open door and nodded. Up we climbed towards the roof, high into the hay and burrowed beneath the cross-beams of the barn. We lay there luxuriously for an hour. Below there was the sound of English voices and then, as the door opened wide, we heard a German talking to the corporal. Through the hay I caught a glimpse of field-grey uniforms. The corporal repeated the word "Nichts!". The German was not satisfied and I felt that he was gazing up into the roof. There was a pause and it seemed that both men went away. There was a sound as if the barn doors were pulled together but not locked and then after a minute came more footsteps and a low whistle. It was the signal that all was well. I saw the corporal was holding up one thumb and grinning. The doors were slammed and there came the turning of the key in the padlock.

We were in the darkness, not daring to speak.

For hours we lay there, listening for sounds outside, and then at ten o'clock we began to remove our khaki battle-dress and bury it in the hay. From old haversacks we drew workmen's clothes which had been smuggled to the camp and rough Polish ski-caps made from Army blankets. Slowly we slid down the mound of hay on to the floor of the barn. The door was difficult to find, but a match quickly extinguished showed us the wire for which we searched. It was loose. The corporal had done his work well. We slid back the wooden bar, gently opened the door, then softly walked out under the stars towards the east.

CHAPTER III

I HEARD the low growl of a dog as we stopped beside a small tree in the slush of the farm yard. Fifty yards away was the outline of the farm-house, now used as a German Officers' Mess. A minute passed and cautiously, one behind the other, we stepped across the soft turf of what seemed to be a garden. This time the dog gave a short bark, and we crouched shivering, by a hedge. A thin column of light appeared in the wall of the farm-house as a door was slowly opened. There was another minute of fearful silence. The door closed again and in the distance we could hear the bolts go home. A wooden fence was before us. We felt carefully with our hands, searching for a foothold to climb over. We lifted ourselves up without noise and saw a great dark mass of trees upon our left and, straight in front, the shade of low hills against the stars. The ground upon the other side of the fence was marshy, and, falling lightly, we began to walk rapidly towards the pale outline of the artillery ground.

In that clear, still night there came no sound of pursuit. I listened for dogs and watched anxiously for the sudden, heartbreaking flash of torches. The glare of arc lamps to the south, betokening another prison camp, was almost friendly. Rapturously I breathed the night breeze as we trod through bushes and heather. The unwonted exercise warmed body and spirit. It was like walking on air. No one who has not known the pain of imprisonment understands the meaning of Liberty.

An hour passed in sheer delight. Up and down through the shell holes we clambered and over a burned heath which crackled beneath our boots. The lights in the south faded to a soft glow of silver, and to the east the line of a new forest appeared, the trees slowly took shape. Along the rides between the trees we marched, without fear, hastening towards the town of Alexandrov twenty miles from the fort.

There came a light at the end of the track and then another; a lantern light it seemed, moving in the breeze. We dashed, panting, into the shade of young fir trees and crouched there, waiting. There was no sound except the wind in the fir trees. The amber lights did not move towards us.

Stepping in and out of cart ruts, stumbling over small piles of newly chopped wood on the edge of the forest, we came to a clearing. Cottages clustered on either side of the track and oil lamps in one of them illumined the rough roadway. In silence we trod in single file along the grass beside the track and passed the foremost of the cottages. There came a staccato, terrifying bark. A door creaked on its hinges and then came another light, very close to us. We ran into the forest, not daring to look to the right or the left, and lay there breathless for many minutes before we moved.

I was carrying a heavy sack of tinned food and chocolate. It began to irk me and cut into my shoulder. Perspiration covered my body beneath Red Cross underclothes of exceptional thickness. My thin Polish workman's jacket and trousers were wet with dew and my feet swelled in the heat of my brown army boots.

When we had covered ten miles, we rested awhile on the grass at a junction of the forest tracks. It was nearly half-past four and the wind grew colder, bringing heavy raindrops. Listening, I heard no more than the sound of my own jaws, munching a bar of chocolate which tasted sour in my mouth. I tried an apple to assuage the bitter-sweet thirst and lay back with my mouth open to catch the slowly falling raindrops. We slung our sacks over sore shoulders and moved on, the tins of sardines and condensed milk rattling as we groped our way.

Sardines and condensed milk! No one who has ever been reduced to such a diet is likely to forget it. These were the pioneer days of 1941 when escaping was not a science but an emotional outburst. I thought of an escape as a kind of hiking tour. In later years, a more finished operation was prescribed by experts, the emphasis being on rapid travel with the minimum of luggage. Even walking became un-fashionable, and jumping a train to the frontier with a mere bar of chocolate in the pocket was all the rage. Concentrated pills of energising food, special drugs to keep the traveller awake, and water-purifying tablets, were supplied. Elaborate maps marked with routes like A.A. tours signalled the advance of new methods. In 1941 there were lessons to be learned and as for Forbes and myself, we were tramps or hoboes, glad to be at large.

Among the clustering pines the road began to rise and then descend until, with our compass pointing south-east, we reached the railway between Podgorz and Sluzewo, a few miles from Alexandrov and over a hundred and fifty from Warsaw. It was a wet and misty dawn. Looking along the railway line I could see the figure of a man moving near a plate-layer's hut. We watched, lying on the edge of the embankment, and felt the rain begin to fall heavily again as the man took shelter. Scrambling down the embankment, we crossed to the other side of the track, where the forest still grew thickly. Light began to dawn towards the end of the trees, and in another two miles these ceased altogether. Ahead there was the faint grey gleam of a road. At eight o'clock on the first morning of our escape, we crept to a signpost on the main road from Thorn to Alexandrov. We had covered nearly twenty miles from the barn.

The road held many perils for us. Even at that early hour German motor vehicles were passing and German nationals or *Volksdeutschen* travelled in carts. There were no Poles, nor did we hear the Polish language. Tramping through the sodden fields not far from the road, out of sight of Ger-man cars, we soon reached the outskirts of Alexandrov. Its white houses were for the most part shuttered and the town was quiet. We skirted its boundaries and set off towards the river bank. A long, straight road with scarcely a tree beside it led endlessly into the mist, towards the town of Nieszawa, beside the Vistula. The rain fell harder yet, forming muddy pools. My thin workmen's clothes were soaked and the skin of my thighs was sore with the motion of walking.

We struggled on, in great misery, the water dripping from our Polish ski-caps down our cheeks, striving against the wind and the downpour until, gasping, we reached a farm-house which bore a Polish name on a narrow label above the door. A woman stared at us from a window. She smiled awkwardly and, opening the window, called to us in Polish against the roar of the rain.

We entered this bare and dirty place where two young sallow-faced women were the only inmates save for a tiny baby in a rough wooden cradle. Both women spoke a little German. They sat beside their kitchen table unmoved and without interest, while we dried all our clothes before an open fire. We seemed neither to attract nor to surprise them as we walked stark naked round the kitchen. We could not explain from where we had come, but the younger of the women, bronze-faced and gypsy, made motions with her arms, as if of swimming. I suppose that they thought we had swum the Vistula. When the time had come to go I watched their humble, frightened faces at the door as we turned for a moment in the rain then went our way.

At noon the storm was over for a time and, in my exhaustion, it seemed as if I were on some dream journey amid little farms and orchards reached by mud paths. A four-wheeled open carriage passed us, driven by a German farmer in flat cap, smoking a short cigar. His arrogant, fleshy face, as it turned to watch us, bore an expression of savage contempt for Poles, and he fingered the stock of his long whip. Then he touched the backs of his two trim chestnut horses and trotted into the distance turning back more than once to watch us. We were afraid of his interest in us. We stood for a moment and hurriedly studied our battered map, then left the road, striking through swamps and flooded paths towards the south-east, in the direction of Wlocawek (Leslau). We were soon lost and bewildered in a maze of poorly cultivated fields and marshy ground. At intervals we stopped to study the sodden map. White crosses, surmounted by rusty Polish helmets stood beneath the trees where spring flowers bloomed. Farmhouses and sheds lay in black ruins, flooded by rain, and a smashed chapel stood with half a crucifix hung above its doorway. This was Hitler's route to Warsaw in the autumn of 1939. Here the Hun had passed by twenty months ago.

We dared not ask for shelter until nightfall and then only when we were sure that the farm was Polish. In nearly every farm-house, however small and mean, were German farmers transplanted by Hitler. In the farm yards, deep in rain and mud, stood fierce mastiffs chained to the walls.

Hopelessly lost among the maze of cart tracks we came to a farm which stood alone and bore a Polish name. An old man in high Polish boots and short black leather jerkin leaned against the fence of a pigsty. We spoke to him in German and asked him the way to Wlocawek. He smiled wisely, touched his high cap of black astrakhan, then spoke in English.

"Good luck." He looked round towards the farm in fear.

"The man here, he is a Tscherman. I work for him, but he is very bad. You must go."

There was another German farmer beside a cow shed. He was thick-set with an evil-tempered red face like the man who had driven past us. He too carried a long black whip and smoked a short cigar. We hurried away from him down a slippery path into the valley and heard him shouting to the Pole as if to a dog.

It was dusk when we walked up the drive of a white farm-house and knocked. A woman opened the door, holding a lamp above her head. She was tall and well built, and spoke to us in Polish asking, so it seemed, anxious questions which we could not understand. She vanished into the darkness of the house and returned with her father and sister. The father looked at us with dreamy blue eyes and stroked his ginger moustache. He had the air of a philosopher and a fanatic and spoke a little German. We made ourselves understood to him, and he took us with the women to the living-room where we stood in silence eyeing each other furtively. I pointed to my torn and soaked trousers of thin cloth and asked the old man if he could help me to find others. He spoke to one of his daughters. She disappeared to another part of the house and came back bringing with her peasant trousers of strong corduroy material. I felt a glow

41

of gratitude, and I shook the father warmly by the hand. Eagerly I examined the trousers.

"But they have no fly buttons!" I exclaimed.

There was laughter. The girls blushed under their tanned faces and quickly I began to cut the buttons off my old trousers with a knife and gave them to the elder daughter. Giggling slyly, she sewed them on to the corduroy.

We sat there until it was dark and heard the rain, returning, beating against the windows. I watched the faces of the girls in the lamplight. They were no longer smiling. The room was heavy with their fear. The farm-house clock ticked loudly on the wall beside the photograph of a dead relative gazing from the shadows. I knew that the girls were watching for a glimpse of field-grey and silver at the window. The lamp flickered ominously with the buffeting of the storm outside. Suddenly there was the sound of heavy boots splashing in the rain and a loud knock. The farmer pointed to the kitchen and we hurried behind its door and stood motionless in the dark. I could hear the bolts of the front door pulled and the hinges creak. I thought of the agonised waiting of the girls at the table. The storm tore fiercely through the open door in gusts so that I had to strain my ears to hear the voices. Swiftly there came relief. The visitor was Polish.

We came back into the lamplight and saw a tall young peasant standing beside the farmer. They were talking quietly and the note of fear in their voices was painful to me. A great feeling of guilt ran through me as I witnessed their terror. Was it to destroy these simple lives that I escaped? Was it not better to endure the bitter frustrations of the Fort, to suffer the enforced companionship of despondent men, all the degradation of being a prisoner? What did it matter whether I escaped or not if others were to die?

I looked at Forbes and wondered what he was thinking. Should we, worn and blistered, renounce their shelter and stumble forth into the night?

The farmer turned to us. He seemed calmer now.

"You sleep in the barn tonight. Go away before dawn. The German farmer here is looking for you."

We were too tired to say more and he led us to a dark barn, and there among the hay we lay down in utter exhaustion. It was cold despite the hay and we slept fitfully

42

until the first cocks crew. A deep grey showed through the gaps in the walls of the barn. In the half-light we searched desperately for Forbes' watch among the hay and then, unsuccessful, cautiously opened the door, tiptoed up the drive and along the road.

As it grew light a man in a tweed jacket and high boots, walking with his bicycle, joined us and spoke to us in Polish. We could not reply. He spoke again in German:

"Where are you walking to?"

"Leslau." (Wlocawek).

"From where?"

"Bromberg."

"What—on foot!"

"Yes."

"Are you *Volksdeutschen*?"

"Yes."

"Then why have you not been called up for service? You look young."

"They will catch up with us yet. We are going to look for work in Leslau."

The man laughed. He looked at us cynically and without belief; then, mounting his bicycle, began to ride unsteadily among the wheel-ruts of the lane. Twice he turned back as the farmer with the chestnut horses had done the previous day.

"That man will certainly report us. Let us break off through these woods and lie up for an hour or so," said Forbes.

Now the sun had risen on the second morning of our escape and the countryside was no longer bare but green and comforting. The blisters on my feet boiled and smarted as if my boots were filled with hot cinders. We sat beside a little stream where crystal water flowed over white stones and quenched our thirst. I took off my boots and bathed my feet, then took from my pocket a pair of scissors and Elastoplast. How strange it seemed to be using homely Elastoplast on such a journey! I husbanded it carefully, examined a tired grey face in a splinter of looking glass, and began to shave laboriously.

Towards three o'clock we saw the towers and factory chimneys of Wlocawek. The town stands upon the huge Vistula which glides past in a muddy flow. Beneath its banks lie layers of shingle littered with sordid rubbish. A mile from the town we sat upon the shingle, tired and once more thirsty. As we lapped the brown water, a dead calf floated past us, bloated and obscene. I turned round at the sound of movement. A German officer was standing on the grass of the bank, hands upon his hips, staring down at us through black-rimmed spectacles. His eyes were puzzled. He seemed about to speak, then walked away over the fields towards Wlocawek. Frightened, we climbed up the bank and walked through the town. Nazi flags and pennants hung from every house and shop and beyond, in the outskirts, from the doorways of low workmen's dwellings. It was Hitler's birthday.

In front of us a Polish Jew, an old bent man, with the star of David painted in yellow on his back, walked slowly on the pavement. A small party of S.S. marched past singing, their arrogant young faces scorning all around them. Hands were raised obediently in the Nazi salute by Poles and German nationals. We, too, saluted with a feeling of tired amusement.

The old Jew, too bent and frail to notice the S.S., shuffled on and did not raise his hand. A fair young thug stepped from the ranks and struck him on the head. His hat spun in the wind and rolled across the road. The S.S. man pushed him from the pavement so that he stumbled in the gutter and began to moan. I saw the hat lying in the mud. No one dared to pick it up.

Once more at dusk we tried to shelter at a farm. A fat blonde woman asked suspiciously:

"Are you *Reichsdeutschen*?"

A youth in a brown shirt looked over his shoulder. I saw his belt—the swastika design and "*Gott mitt uns*" around it. We were again amongst the enemy. We turned away as the Germans stood staring, and hurried to the edge of a great forest stretching in to the far distance along the banks of the Vistula. We sank among the pine needles as it grew dark. I could go no further, each foot was a great, sore, smouldering mass and each step a separate agony. The moon began to rise among the trees as we huddled together and tried to rest, and through the night there came the grunting of wild boars.

On the morning of the third day of our escape we continued slowly towards higher ground along the south bank of the Vistula meeting here and there a lonely woodman. I could travel at only a very slow pace. It seemed that I had lost my feet and that my legs were only raw stumps, dragging along the ground. Sometimes we lay down in the sun to sleep fitfully in a clearing and caught a sudden view of the Vistula below us as the clouds parted. In the afternoon, descending steep sandy hills, we went over the railway line that crosses the river from the town of Plock on its north bank, and made for Gombin. It was evening when we reached it, a long, straggling village, deserted and unfriendly.

We trod the road to Warsaw in the cool sunset hoping that perhaps this night we should find shelter. In the distance, dark woods seemed to welcome us, but like mirages in a desert, turned into plantations of young trees where no shelter could be found. We stumbled back south of the road and there lay down in the furrows of a ploughed field, sheltering beneath a fold in the ground, trying to sleep.

I thought the night would never end. Every hour the great cold made us rise and shake ourselves to be certain that we were alive. Our stock of chocolate was exhausted and only the condensed milk and the sardines remained. The utter nausea of this mixture will remain with me to the end of my days.

At daybreak on the fourth day, we set off without breakfast over a huge expanse of ploughed land, determined to reach Warsaw that night. The cold numbed the pain of my blistered feet as I trod the hard furrows, and regaining the road, we walked to the town of Itow, thirty miles from Warsaw. Lines of farm carts stood in the main street as we made towards the frontier of the General Government of Poland. This was the area of Polish Territory that formed a buffer state between the Russians and the western lands restored to German nationals.

With only rough maps to guide us we were doubtful of the position of the frontier. Three miles beyond Itow, we came to another small down-trodden village. We saw a woman at a garden gate and shamelessly asked for the frontier.

"It is here," she cried excitedly, and frightened, disappeared among a flock of chattering geese.

45

Tiredness and pain overcame any sense of caution. We walked straight through the village and turned a slight bend in the road. Before us were white-painted frontier posts and a gate, open and inviting. Beside it was a guard house. No sentries, no controls, no sign of life.

We walked through the posts and, undecided, stepped off the roadway onto the grass making for a new patch of forest. Two German frontier guards, a bare twenty yards away, sat together upon a bank watching us in silence. Their rifles lay beside them. They picked them up and walked towards us as we stood, worn out and unable to run away. They were big and stupid and fresh-faced and spoke to us amiably as British constables would address a pair of tramps.

"Where are your papers?"

Forbes did the talking for he spoke the best German.

"We have none."

They looked at us in surprise.

"Everyone must have papers to cross the General-Government frontier. Surely you know that?"

"But we were only going to visit our mother who is sick at Sochaczew. This is my brother," said Forbes, indicating me.

I smiled faintly.

"Where have you come from?"

"Gombin."

"We can soon check up on that, my children."

They led us back to the guard house and pushed open the door of a small office where a hard-faced man sat at a table with a heavy leather whip hanging from the wall beside him. His hair was rumpled and his tunic unbuttoned at the neck. Behind him on a bed slept another German. The man at the table looked up and shouted at us as we stood awkwardly by the door.

"Attention, Polish swine!"

We stood painfully to attention, and listened to the sentry's report of our discovery. The official stared at us with crazy bloodshot eyes. He told the sentries to take Forbes outside the door and wait. I stood before the table, trying to answer his questions. I told him that I was a *Volksdeutsch* from the Bromberg district. In my terrible fatigue, my brain refused to function clearly. I forgot my German and spoke to him haltingly. He began to laugh and brandished the whip in my face. I tried to maintain my story, hoping that Forbes would get the chance to break away outside. I could not. I no longer cared that I was caught again or even if this brutal official were to flog me to death. I struggled with his questions for a few minutes and then unable to fight on showed him my metal identity disc with my name and the words "Prisoner of War No. 1198."

They brought Forbes back and the man on the bed woke up and joined in the chorus of threats. For several minutes Forbes struggled gallantly with their cross-examination.

"We don't believe you! You are not Englishmen, but Polish spies! This is a matter for the Gestapo."

The man at the table lifted the telephone receiver and began to talk rapidly. I did not hear. I swayed half-fainting against the wall of the guard-house and every time I did so the man on the bed told me sharply to stand to attention.

I heard the telephone ringing again and it seemed that the officials had become less harsh. A sentry came to the door, and we were ordered to march back with him to Itow. The sentry was a friendly man and did not hurry us, and, as we walked painfully in front of him, Forbes tore a piece of paper in small bits. With the morning sunlight I felt less tired and remembered in an instant what it was. We had provided ourselves with two copies of a map of the German aerodrome at Graundenz. A great fear surged through me, hopeless as I was. Where was the other copy?

From the Police Station at Itow, we were taken in the back of a truck with one sentry to guard us along the road we had travelled the day before until, reaching the great forest, we came to a pontoon bridge over the Vistula, beside the black skeleton of a suspension bridge. The town of Plock, on the north bank, seemed to me a dull, cheerless place filled with dejected Poles and S.S. men strutting in the streets. There was saluting everywhere from Poles and Germans alike.

The truck drew up beside a high modern stone building and we were ordered down to the pavement. The sentry moved with us towards the entrance and, as he did so, my heart missed a beat, then pounded in my throat. Upon a notice board beside the entrance was the word:

GESTAPO.

A wooden hatch was lifted and a grim face appeared. We

were hustled to a small room and stood there waiting. A burly man in S.S. uniform came through the door, pushing me to one side so that I nearly fell against the wall, and passed into an office. Then came a man in plain clothes with blond hair and a pale, cruel face. He shouted at us to remove everything from our pockets. We emptied crushed and broken bits of bread and chocolate, parts of maps, a box of matches concealing a small compass, and laid them on the table before him. He looked at these objects with disgust and without interest. Then, suddenly, he unfolded a small bit of paper from my wallet. I watched in horror— it was the missing map of Graudenz aerodrome.

"So! my friends, you are from the Secret Service!"

They took us separately to a room upstairs where a young S.S. officer in uniform began to fire questions at me in English. His manner was curt and nervous. He offered me a cigarette, and as I answered his questions I heard a typewriter behind me tap out my replies.

He interrogated me closely about our escape from the camp, and about the plan of the aerodrome. My story was that we had got the plan from other prisoners working near Graudenz. We had planned to escape by stealing an aircraft from that aerodrome, since Forbes was a pilot.

The young German did not smile.

"You are lying. You are a spy. You were taking this to the Russians."

"No, we were not. We were trying the same game as the three Canadian pilots who the other day climbed into an aircraft to fly to Sweden."

He had not heard of this attempt, but listened carefully. I told him of their escape, giving no more away than the Germans knew at Thorn. Then relieved, I heard him ring up Thorn and confirm the story. The S.S. man seemed to believe me. He smiled a little and we began to talk of the war. Another S.S. man joined us and, talking in German, we studied a map on the wall. Soon I noticed that the typewriters were silent and that the typists were standing by us listening, enthralled by our conversation. I tried to persuade them that England could still win the war. They laughed cynically, then turned the subject to Poland, trying to discover whether we had been helped by any of the peasants. I parried the thrust asking them:

"Why do you treat the Poles so harshly?"

"Because the Fuehrer says so."

There was a Catholic emblem on the wall.

"If you are Catholics, why do you smash their crucifixes and persecute their priests?"

"Because sub-human beings have no need of religion."

I looked at the fair young man who had interrogated me first. I was no longer afraid of him or that I should be treated as a spy. My confidence returned.

"Please tell me what you were doing before all this began."

He blushed.

"I was taking my doctorate of philosophy at the University," he said angrily.

He turned on his heel and pressed a bell. A great gorilla of a man in plain clothes and a drawn revolver entered the room. The young philosopher spoke to me again, harsh and embarrassed.

"You are going to prison now. You will be shot if you try to escape."

I walked with the gorilla in silence through the streets of Plock and came to a severe modern prison with the forbidding title of *Strafgefängnis* where I was joined by Forbes. Our clothes and what remained of our belongings were taken from us and we were given grey prison garments that felt like boards against the skin. They separated me from Forbes and I was led up iron stairs to a gallery on one side of the prison. Around me was the clink of keys, the slamming of doors, and harsh shouts sounding the length of the great building, just as I heard them at Nuremberg four years after. The warder opened the door of a cell on the second floor and gave orders:

"Take your boots off!"

I did as I was told, slowly and painfully, while the warder stood staring at me. I put my boots outside the door, which slammed loudly, then lay upon a hard mattress and slept dreamlessly until the evening.

When I awoke, there was a noise outside as of some metal object being drawn across the iron floor of the gallery. The keys turned in the lock and the door opening, revealing a Polish boy in prison clothes dragging a great container filled with soup. I snatched a tin bowl from one corner of my cell and he filled it, whispering to me in German all the while. Sometimes he looked round fearfully for the warder who was busy opening doors along the gallery.

"You are English," said the boy. "I know. They are talking about it in the kitchen. We poor Poles are waiting for the day of victory." His eyes glistened. "We have suffered enough."

He could say no more and dragged away the steaming container. I lifted the bowl to my mouth and greedily drank a tasteless swill of bad potatoes and swedes.

As it grew dark in the cell I heard confused sounds of traffic in the road below. There were loud cries from one of the cells as of a man in agony.

If I could have seen into the future, I should have seen another cell, close to Keitel's on that October afternoon in 1945 at Nuremberg. In that cell stood a dark man with sneering mouth. He was Hans Frank, Hitler's governor of occupied Polish territories—the Butcher of Poland. I was now in his territory and within his power.

Frank was the man who, as Hitler's chief legal adviser, first debased the law by developing the thesis that it was subordinate only to the Party. Later he became the organiser of slaughter and persecution on a huge scale. He was responsible for the liquidation in Poland of nearly two million human beings. He was the man to whom jackbooted S.S. and brutal cigar-smoking German farmers owed loyalty.

As I stood in Frank's cell four years later, I remembered the prison at Plock. I remembered when I looked at his right arm swathed in black cloth to hide his wrist, paralysed by the cutting of an artery when he attempted suicide. I remembered when he moaned with self-pity and pretended remorse. Within five days of my handing him his copy of the indictment, he was received into the Roman Catholic Church which he had once forsaken for the pagan philosophy of Nazism.

Through the trial, I listened to the recital of his crimes among the Polish people. What I remembered of Poland was the smashed chapel in the rainstorm and half a crucifix hung above the doorway. And now Hans Frank was restored to a Church he had thought unfit for Poles.

The keys were silent in the prison of Plock and I slept until a blue sky showed through the tiny barred window and the warder flung my boots at me from the open door.

CHAPTER IV

THE cell occupied by the sneering Butcher of Poland at Nuremberg differed little in appearance and size from my cell in the prison of Plock. For two whole days I slept on my hard bed waking only to eat bread and turnip soup and for half an hour each day to take exercise in the courtyard. During the exercise the prisoners stood in two ranks doing gymnastics and then ran in a circle followed by warders waving sticks. Two of the inmates were priests in cassocks who stumbled and fell. Another prisoner, a poor lunatic with a long mane of hair, ran in the wrong direction chased by a great sadist of a warder. Forbes and myself, still with blistered feet not yet healed, were permitted to walk apart from the other inmates. Conversation was forbidden but in whispers we were able to discuss the story we had already told the Gestapo about the plan of Graudenz aerodrome north-east of Thorn. I found, to my relief, that Forbes had already given a similar account. We had previously agreed to tell the Gestapo that, after leaving the dentist's hut, we had straightway crossed the road between the Kommandantur and the compound of Stalag XXa, and escaped into the forest. We denied that we had ever hidden among British soldiers.

One afternoon the warder opened the door at an unusual hour.

"The Gestapo wants you," he said curtly, jangling his bunch of keys, and handed me over to a waiting escort, a tall S.S. man who led me through the streets of Plock.

Trembling, I climbed the steps with him to the Gestapo building and entered a new office on the first floor, where a man in civilian clothes sat alone at a desk. He had a scar across his cheek and close-cut, dark hair. A Polish woman stood in front of him in grey prison dress. I saw her bare feet as she stood to attention in Polish fashion with the palms of her hands against her thighs. The toenails of her feet were dirty and broken and the skin was rough as if accustomed to hard usage. She was a working woman, bony and sallow, but looking with splendid defiance at the creature at the desk. Here was a woman who would never surrender. When her interrogation was finished, she was led away by other S.S. guard. I caught her eye and smiled. The man at the desk was furious.

"Go on, smile at her, English officer. You started this war. You brought these Poles into it. Both of you are spies! spies! spies!" he cried hysterically.

I felt the perspiration on my face and neck and I trembled as I stood before the desk. I could not speak. He watched me for a full minute with murder in his pale grey eyes. Then he spoke again slowly. There was a slow menace in his voice.

"We are not satisfied with this sketch. This plan of the aerodrome has come from a Pole. Where did you get it?"

"I have told you. I got it from another prisoner of war."

"Name?" he demanded.

"I will not tell you."

"All right, English gentleman, you stay with the Gestapo until you think better of your obstinacy."

He watched me closely with his mad eyes. Suddenly he said something in a different tone which, despite my terror, filled me with a certain detached astonishment. I had not thought of him as capable of human feelings.

"You need not think, Lieutenant Neave, that because I am in civilian clothes I have not seen fighting like yourself. I was in the Polish campaign last year, and was wounded." He pointed to a small yellow and white ribbon in the buttonhole of his coat.

"Go, Herr Neave, and think things over."

I was led back to the main door of the *Strafgefängnis* and at the entrance was left to stand before a group of Polish prisoners. There I remained for over half an hour. I became impatient, despite my fear, and said to a warder:

"I am an English officer. Why am I standing here?"

The man turned round, surprised, and shouted furiously, "We need no officers here!"

The Poles, murderers, thieves and other criminals, grinned broadly and gave me a look of friendly recognition until the warder brandished his stick at them. Then I was hurriedly taken to my cell and saw upon the door the notice:

I lay upon my bed, too frightened even to move. With every noise outside the cell there shot through me an intense pang of fear. First I prayed, then I cursed and paced about the cell. I knew that once in the hands of the Gestapo, there was small hope of any return to the German High Command which administered the camp at Thorn. From the Army alone there was hope of military justice. No one knew what happened to the victims of the Gestapo. When the "evening meal" appeared, the Polish boy smiled at me sadly as he ladled out the soup.

"You are going tomorrow."

There was no time to ask him more. The warder came and hurried him away. I watched the shadows lengthen in the cell and, when the doors opened once more for the prisoners to put their boots and outer clothes outside, I stood for a moment looking across the gallery. There, in his doorway, stood a Polish officer under sentence of death for killing a Gestapo agent. He smiled and bowed politely from the other side. I bowed in return. It seemed that we were about to tread the same path.

I thought of Forbes. Was he also afraid? Had he been able to tell the same story as I, and had they believed him? Were they, by calling us spies, trying to frighten us into some admission that we had been helped by the Poles? I felt almost a longing to return to the custody of the stupid bourgeois German Army officers on the staff at Stalag XXa. The university graduates of the Gestapo were evil and dangerous, and without humanity. I seemed to hear the typewriter endlessly tapping out the statements that would be used against me. I struggled in a web of terror and speculation. Surely an Intelligence Officer could only draw one conclusion from our possession of the Graudenz plan, for Graudenz was to the north of Thorn, whilst we were stopped on the road to Warsaw walking towards the Russian lines.

I closed my eyes, and despair came over me like a great fog. I could not see a way out of the darkness, not one gleam of light. I was lost on a great moorland where the mist came down and hid every landmark. I dreamed that I was once more tramping through swamps of dark, stagnant, water on the road to Russia. Torrents rushed across my path into the gloom and I came to higher ground, passing upon the way the bones of former travellers. The mists cleared, revealing a summer's day, and I was once more among the Essex fields of my childhood. It was my first journey from the station, sitting in a yellow dog-cart in a sailor suit. The wheels spun in the dust of the lane and as the dog-cart reached white gates, the old groom leapt down to open them. Up the drive we trotted and halted before a cracked conservatory and there was the murmur of summer flies and bees. I was lifted down and someone took my hand in theirs and led me up white steps. I heard a soft ringing sound of boots on an iron scraper before we stepped into the hall.

As I awoke from this early memory the sound of the scraper became that of the eternal prison keys. The sun was shining in the cell and the door was open. I braced myself to meet Death. The warder stood there. He did not throw my boots at me but only said with unwonted friendliness:

"Get dressed, Herr Leutnant. You are going back to Thorn with your comrade, the Oberleutnant of the R.A.F."

Herr Oberleutnant and Herr Leutnant! We were no longer spies. Springing from the bed, I seized my clothes and boots in wild delight, and dressed as if it were the first day of the school holidays. Then came the *ersatz* coffee and a hunk of bread, and I was led to the office of the prison where Forbes was waiting. We greeted each other excitedly, as men do in moments of escape from danger.

Our reinstatement as officers changed the attitude of the prison staff towards us. Even the sourest of the officials seemed polite. They were surprised at these two smiling Englishmen, until yesterday within the clutches of the dreaded Gestapo. I watched them at their desks. I could see the astonishment on their faces as they listened to the representatives of a country whose capital Hitler claimed to have destroyed and whose surrender all Germany expected.

In the prison store we were handed back our escaping clothes in exchange for the convict uniform. A few tins of condensed milk and sardines still remained in the old sack. Jokingly, I gave the gloomy prison quartermaster a piece of Red Cross chocolate. He looked at it as if it were a jewel, then stuck it furtively in the pocket of his tunic and put his fingers to his lips. He returned my pipe, tobacco and the box of matches. I opened the matchbox to light my pipe and there beneath the matches was the compass. Incomprehensibly, the Gestapo, though they found it, had put it back and sent it to the prison with our other belongings.

The train from Plock to Thorn travelled slowly along the flat north bank of the Vistula. We sat beside our guards on wooden seats and talked to them about the war. Our opinion left them sitting dumb and open-mouthed, and even shocked. We knew more than they did, for within the fort at Thorn there was a closely guarded wireless receiving set beneath the boards of my room, which someone had smuggled in a medicine ball from Spangenburg.

It was evening when we reached the fort, still limping from blisters, and hoping to be restored to our old rooms and companions, but a grim night was before us. At the guardroom was an angry *Feldwebel* who had been in charge of the guards from whom we escaped. He welcomed us with anger and injured pride. Amid the usual shouts, the remaining tins of sardines and condensed milk were seized and flung in a corner. Drawing his revolver, the *Feldwebel* led us, with our hands above our heads, into the chill blackness of the moat. His torch shone on two semi-circular chambers in the outer wall, used as a store for rotting swedes and timber. The doors were of sheet iron each with a circular hole cut in the face, the only windows. Within, there was the odour of vegetable decay, and on the floor a few old sacks to serve as bedding. The *Feldwebel* locked us in separate chambers and stamped off along the moat, swearing as he went. We had escaped the Gestapo, but our insult to the German Army must now be expurgated.

I lay on the sacks and tried to sleep. The dense, foul smell of rotting swedes drove me every hour to the circle of air in the iron door. It was cold, and through the night I paced the earthen floor of the narrow chamber. Only in the centre could I stand upright. At the sides, I was forced to bend my head beneath the curved brick roof. Sometimes, tiring of this manoeuvre, I sat on a pile of swedes which rolled and tumbled beneath me, or leant against the arch of the wall, my head bent nearly to my chin. My position was too painful for reflection upon my adventures of the past few days, but I could at least give thanks that I was no longer in the power of Heinrich Himmler, Reichsfuehrer of the S.S. and Gestapo, though I would have given much for the comparative comfort of my prison bed at Plock.

Unable to rest, I stood before the hole in the door, stamping my feet, until the blackness of the moat turned to grey and voices came from the red brick walls opposite. Faces appeared and filled the windows and there was shouting across the moat. I could hear Forbes calling from next door in loud protest against our filthy prisons. Then a coarse voice spoke aloft. A passing sentry on the edge of the moat pointed his rifle downwards so that the barrel appeared before the hole in the door close to my face.

"If you are swine hounds you must expect to be kept in pigsties," remarked the sentry.

"I will report your filthy language to the Kommandant," I said.

The rifle disappeared immediately, for a German can always be disarmed by the threat of trouble with his superiors, even from the inmate of a pigsty.

When we were both half crazy from cold and hunger and exasperation, the iron doors were opened and we were taken again along the moat to a room in a kind of keep at the head of the drawbridge. This was a room without furniture except for two beds and a stove, where we slept quietly, physically and emotionally exhausted.

As our strength returned, we began to ponder, not without self-recrimination, upon the failure of our escape. There could only be one conclusion. We had attempted to cross this wild, cheerless land at too fast a pace and without method. We had, as it were, charged the barricade of the General-Government frontier without calculation. It was now clear that it would have been comparatively simple to skirt it through the surrounding woods and make our way to hiding in Warsaw. In such a stern, sparse country the escaper must be warned of the strains upon the spirit. Loneliness and physical stress undermine the most resolute. He must conserve his forces by lying up for long periods where he can keep warm, if only in a haystack or in a leafy thicket.

When we were released, quiet days passed in our rooms in the fort, describing our experiences and writing veiled allusions to them in our letters home. I found myself refreshed and invigorated by my few days of freedom. I turned to reading books which brought an inner peace and sense of home—solid Victorian novels provided by the Red Cross, and even the *Law Quarterly Review*.

It was the night I finished *East Lynne* that there came a noise at the head of my bed which woke me about three o'clock. I opened my eyes to see a huge German shining a torch at me. The torch light faintly illuminated his eyes and a front gold tooth. Beneath the outline of his helmet he was a disturbing vision.

"Get up and be ready to move immediately. We have had enough trouble with you."

I dressed in complete darkness amid sleepy snatches of conversation from my room mates. They were gloomy about my future. Was I to be sent back to Plock? Were the Army surrendering me to the philosophers of the Gestapo?

There were lights on the drawbridge as I was led there through the passages of the fort, and shadowy figures stamped their feet, talking in English and even laughing. I recognised Forbes, Squadron Leader Paddon and Lieutenant-Commander Stephenson, R.N., who, a short time before, had tried to escape in a dust cart and involved themselves in violent altercation with the *Feldwebel* at the gate. Each of us carried a small bundle as we stood waiting in the cold night air to be taken from the fort.

"Where in hell are we going?" I exclaimed.

"To the Bad Boys' Camp at Colditz."

I did not know where Colditz was, nor would the Germans tell us.

So strong was the atmosphere of school which influenced our lives that the idea of a camp for naughty boys, a sort of Borstal, caused me no surprise. I was greatly flattered that so early in my prison career I should be singled out as a nuisance to the enemy. I was like a boy, who, flogged by the headmaster, proudly displays the stripes on his backside. And, as we crossed the drawbridge for the last time, I looked forward to new adventures.

East Lynne had quietened a mind feverishly groping for new plans of escape. A journey by train, however, was an opportunity which no one could resist. On this May morning, I watched the dawn break over the countryside from the windows of the express to the Bad Boys' Camp. We changed trains at the big railway station of Posen, and, as we stood on the platform, a man spat viciously at us. Each prisoner was alert and ready for the slightest chance to get away, but we were heavily guarded, even in the lavatory. We were already looked on as incorrigible escapers and the location of the Bad Boys' Camp was carefully concealed from us.

The guard who sat beside me in the train from Posen to Dresden was a talkative lower middle-class character with grey hair and the inevitable gold front tooth. He had a foolish well-meaning face and seemed to be just the sort of person to work upon and soften up. He said that he kept a little toy-shop near Dresden which he had had to leave for military service. He bored me with his toy business but I talked to him so feelingly that tears came into his stupid blue eyes. He understood, he said, what it was to be far from home. I exploited his kindliness without shame in the hope of jumping off the train or giving him the slip when we reached Dresden.

There is a fascination in the waiting-room of a big station such as Dresden in the early hours of the morning. It is then that the traveller may study the German people at close quarters as they try to sleep or talk in hushed whispers while they eat thick sandwiches of bread and sausages. We prisoners of war sat at tables beside our guards, attracting no attention. Soon both guards and prisoners began to fall asleep, their heads resting on their elbows on the marble-topped tables. At intervals, officials of the railway police in dark blue uniforms walked round the tables demanding papers, and once or twice led off cringing travellers.

The toy-shop keeper and I went on talking about the war, and what would happen when it was all over. Unlike the usual dull-faced Germans to whom we were accustomed as guards, this man had much that was interesting to tell, and he did not seem to be afraid to do so. He spoke of the Communists in Dresden and said that if Hitler were defeated there would be many Brown shirts which would change to Red.

As he talked on, I watched the doors of the waiting-room. The sentries' rifles lay on the floor beside them. Only one, an under-officer, carried a revolver and he was dreaming peacefully. The toy-shop keeper unbuttoned his tunic and rose to his feet. He beckoned me over to a screen behind which a group of railway workers were drinking coffee. He introduced me to the men who were friendly and surprisingly responsive to seditious propaganda. The toy-shop keeper asked me for my address at home in case, he said, we should meet again after the war. I would gladly have obtained his address to blackmail him into letting me escape, but he was too cautious.

The time was passing quickly and I must soon make an attempt to dash through the crowded waiting-room, out on to the platform and into the streets of Dresden. I was tired from the strain of waiting for my chance. The toy-shop keeper and the railway workers began to talk among themselves, leaving me leaning against the wall of the waiting-room. I shuffled towards a side door with my back against the wall. When I was within a yard of the door, the toy-shop man turned round and spoke to me. He had not noticed my movement. His gold tooth shone through an irritating smile and he said amiably, as if I were a child selecting a toy.

"More coffee, Englishman?"

I walked over to him angrily, fearing to excite suspicion by refusing, took my cup of coffee and drank with resignation. I could have smacked his foolish bourgeois face, for the chance had gone. In a few minutes civilians were yawning in the waiting-room and we followed them on to the platform to take the train to our new prison camp.

I often think of the toy-shop man, for he was sincere in his hatred of war and his sympathy for my misfortune, and now I feel almost ashamed of my attempt to take advantage of his good nature. Some time in 1946 I received a letter from him sent to me at the address I had given him in the waiting-room at Dresden. He told me in veiled terms of the new tyranny under which he was suffering in the Eastern Zone of Germany, and asked for my help. There was nothing I could do but reply in terms that would not excite the interest of Communist censors. Some hypocrite has called this the century of the Common Man, but in no age have common men suffered more for being human and kindly.

The train which took us to the Bad Boy's Camp at Colditz, twenty-eight miles from Leipzig, was packed with civilian travellers. In our compartment, a German officer, a *Haupt-*

mann and his wife, sat opposite me. He was a middle-aged person in some administrative unit, short-sighted behind black-rimmed glasses and acutely nervous. He peered at my battledress and then turned to his wife with an expression of protest and warning.

"Kriegsgefangener!"

The effect of his hoarse whisper was to increase my sense of self-importance after months of exclusion from the world of human beings. I did not feel insulted that he intended to convey to me his indignation at being forced to travel in the same compartment as a British prisoner of war.

His wife was called Hilde. She was larger than the *Hauptmann*. Her sexless face, as if carved from wood, was like that of a man disguised for a theatrical performance. I was to see just such a face as this months afterwards at the Bad Boys' Camp. It belonged to a lantern-jawed French officer of awkward gait, clad in a coat and skirt of his own design, who tried to escape as the wife of a camp official. He failed, but his appearance was a splendid tilt at middle-aged German womanhood.

Hilde's eyes were blue and spiteful and mean. Her chin protruded above a thick, red neck and her great breasts swelled beneath her blouse. No amount of enforced celibacy would have aroused any desire for her, but her conversation held my deep attention. She was a great talker, indifferent to the presence of others, and an embarrassment to the Herr *Hauptmann* as he shrank in his corner by the window. I listened to catch every word she said for her subject was indeed fascinating. She was talking of Rudolf Hess. She was annoyed.

"Why?" she asked, "did the Fuehrer not stop him? I do not understand. Where did he get the aeroplane?"

The sentries caught their breath and looked uncomfortable. The *Hauptmann* seeing a gleam of unconcealed interest in my eye, turned to her in pompous fury, and pointed to a notice in the compartment to the effect that the enemy was listening—which indeed he was.

"Hilde, please to remember that we are in the presence of the enemy."

The *Hauptmann* turned towards the window and looked moodily at the Saxon countryside. Hilde breathed heavily, clutching a vast handbag, and looked straight before her.

A broad grin spread over the face of the enemy. I lit my pipe and winked at my fellow-prisoners.

In May, 1941, when we were travelling towards the Bad Boys' Camp at Colditz, the name of Hess was on the lips of every German. As the train jolted on I little thought that four years afterwards I should meet him in his cell at Nuremburg, a half-mad creature, manacled to an American guard. But as the scenery increased in splendour, Hess was forgotten and I wondered what awaited me at the Bad Boys' Camp.

CHAPTER V

THE great castle of Augustus the Strong of Saxony towers above the village of Colditz and from its battlements you can see the River Mulde winding to the east. The castle, grey and immense, keeps watch over the rich countryside. On three sides its walls look down to a sheer precipice of rock, so that it stands impregnable and supreme. Beneath its southern face there is a dry moat over which a bridge leads from the principal gateway to a clock tower at the entrance to the outer courtyard. The eighteenth-century buildings enclosing this courtyard housed in 1941 the German Kommandantur of Oflag IVc., designated a "Special Camp" for wrongdoers of all the Allied nations.

The Inner courtyard of earlier date where dwelt the prisoners in those days is reached by ascending a rampart along a cobbled roadway to a seventeenth-century guardhouse which adjoins its gates. These gates are surmounted by an archway carrying a Bridge of Sighs which connects the guard-house with a block of stone buildings overlooking the rampart. Within the courtyard, walls rise sharply on either side to a height of ninety feet. Of medieval thickness they stand on solid rock, giving to the castle an appearance of formidable strength. Their deep foundations spring from the ruins of earlier fortresses and present a fearsome obstacle to the prisoner who hopes to escape by tunnelling. At each corner of the courtyard are round towers within which steep spiral staircases ascend to lofty rooms which once housed the retinues of past rulers of Saxony. A tall chapel built on the north side in the seventeenth century has along its outer wall a terrace overlooking the precipice below. On the east side the terrace, continuing, descends beside a steep grassy bank to the parkland of the castle. The rooms on this side were, in May, 1941, the quarters of about twenty British officers. The buildings on the south, separating the two courtyards, formed the prisoners' kitchens and canteen while, on the west, high above the grey roofs of Schloss Colditz, French and Polish officers gazed through barred windows to the distant hills or watched a sentry moodily pacing beside his machine-gun in a garden at the front of a parapet.

The eighteenth-century reign of Augustus, dubbed by Carlyle the "Physically Strong" on account of his renowned sexual capacity, was the most eventful period in the history of the castle. With the declining power of Saxon princes it became a lunatic asylum and then a concentration camp for the political opponents of Hitler. The grandeur of the centuries gave way to scenes of madness and brutality within its walls.

In the war, something of the vitality and colour of earlier days returned to the old courtyard. It became the meeting place of Jews, escapers, and "bad boys" from all the nations who had incurred the wrath of the Nazis. The vast domain of princelings was now heavily guarded. Barbed wire and machine-guns bristled on the parapets and even from the slate roofs sentries watched the prisoners below. And, as if to indicate that hygiene had progressed but slowly since the days of Augustus a delousing shed was erected in the western corner of the courtyard. Despite this evidence of the twentieth century, a gay Elizabethan spirit was abroad among the inmates. They sauntered proudly beneath the turrets, conscious that they were regarded by the enemy as specially dangerous. British, French, Belgians, Dutch, Poles and Serbs lived in an atmosphere of genuine companionship, united in a common desire to infuriate the Germans, and, if possible, to escape.

Early one morning at the end of May we marched from the station up a causeway, crossed the moat-bridge and halted at the guard-house. The great gates of the inner courtyard were opened to admit us. I felt the battlements close in, enfolding me, so that I looked round in fear. White faces peered at me from the windows and men in strange clothes paced up and down in the shadows. Then I saw John Hyde-Thomson, sent to the castle after his escape from Thorn, walking in clogs on the cobblestones. His orange high-necked sweater and ancient khaki shorts were a genial challenge to the frowning walls. He came towards me laughing.

John was a regular soldier and a companion of my Oxford days. Slim in build, with long features, his face had originality and character. There was a pleasant shyness in his manner, and he had the temperament of an artist delighting in careless poses which defied the conventions of prison life. Despite his nonchalance, he was a determined escaper. He was one of the pioneers of escaping among the Army officers in the early days at Spangenburg though he was never successful. He died all too soon in Uganda in 1951.

Amid such gaiety and friendship, the lowering prison seemed to recede from my thoughts as men of all nations came out to welcome us in high spirits. It was as if we had escaped from a turgid political meeting to a salon filled with wit and self-confidence, if not with sartorial good taste, so different was Colditz from the depression of Thorn. Among the twenty British officers were no fewer than three clergymen of the Chaplain's department. The Reverend J. Ellison Platt, M.B.E., C.F. and the Reverend J. Hobling, C.F., the latter in clerical collar and clogs, were walking together in the courtyard. Each had the same gay attitude as the other prisoners.

"What are you wicked parsons doing here?" I asked, having known them both at Spangenburg.

"That's what we should like to know."

I elicited no clear reason why either of them should have been branded as Bad Boys by the humourless Germans. They were joined by the Reverend R. G. Heard, M.B.E., M.C., a don at Cambridge, and all three were during my stay at Colditz a source of guidance to the unruly and of consolation to the unpopular and the heavy-laden. It is sad to record that Joe Hobling was killed by an American bomb in another camp later in the war.

The padres led us up a stone staircase to a great hall upon the first floor where all the British lived save for a handful of senior officers. I felt as if I was being ushered by masters to a school for waifs and strays, though in later days the atmosphere often changed to that of a mental home. We sat down like guests at a Tudor feast, to drink stews from tin bowls and eat German bread and lard off the bare boards. The food was well supplemented from the Red Cross supplies of biscuits, jam and chocolate, carefully rationed. When we were fed, we each found beds in two smaller rooms leading from the dining-hall and straightway went to sleep.

Every officer in this castle had but a single thought—to escape. Like all genuine escapers they conformed to no pattern. Many were eccentric and unusual men. Enthusiasm for escaping is a matter of individual character, and most of us in Colditz worked out our own science of escape. Magpie hoards of keys, wire, knives and useful bits of metal were concealed in private "hides" all over the castle. Ancient lead piping was melted down to make German uniform buttons and a dentist's drill employed to fashion false keys. Less technical minds studied languages, copied maps and collected stolen articles of civilian clothing.

It was stimulating to live in this hive of industry. I began to join in escape plans with other officers feeling that I need no longer fear the indulgent smiles of those who were content to lead a vegetable existence in my previous camps.

I played no part in the first big attempt by British officers to escape by tunnel in June 1941. As a newcomer I had no place in this tunnel. Its mouth was beneath the floorboards of the canteen and it ran to a point beyond the outer wall on the eastern side of the castle. A patch of grass sheltered by the walls, grew on a parapet at the foot of which a pathway led into the Park. A sentry stood under the floodlight on the grass and another below the parapet beside the fence of barbed wire bordering the path. The tunnellers, led by the Senior British Officer, Colonel Guy German, D.S.O., planned to escape through the turf and then descend into the Park.

The principal author of this plan was Pat Reid, M.B.E., M.C. He appointed officers who could speak German to select a sentry suitable for bribery with money and chocolate and who would look the other way when the escapers left the exit of the tunnel. They found a genial German soldier who took part in many whispered interviews in doorways and in the shadows of the courtyard. He accepted money, cigarettes and chocolate and agreed to be on duty at the small area of grass on the appointed night.

That night in June the escapers, twelve in number, entered the canteen after the prisoners had paraded for their evening meal. The door of the canteen had already been unlocked by Reid removing the lock on the inside. A confused crowd of officers dispersing to their various doorways shrouded from the Germans the disappearance of the escapers within the canteen. Once inside, the escapers, hidden in the tunnel, waited for Reid to burrow through the last few feet of masonry and earth.

I watched the courtyard from a vantage point in the British quarters and listened. The sentry in the courtyard stood by the delousing shed beneath an arc lamp. He seemed indifferent to the tension of that silent night. I knew that in the castle hearts were beating fiercely and silent prayers were being offered among the Allies for the men who were at that moment crawling in the tunnel. I began to doze before the rusty bars. It was past two o'clock when I woke with a painful start. Loud German voices came from the front gate, brutally disturbing the massive stillness of the castle. I saw figures with rifles rush across the courtyard to the door of the canteen, led by an elderly police officer, an amiable person with a white moustache, known to the prisoners as "Tiger". Brandishing a revolver he called in an excited quavering voice on the inmates of the tunnel to surrender. The months of toil had been in vain. The tunnellers were led sadly away to solitary confinement. They had been betrayed by the sentry thought to be corruptible. He had reported all the negotiations to the Kommandantur.

The result of this episode was that I was placed in charge of the British side of the canteen in place of the former canteen officer, a stockbroker named Kenneth Lockwood of the Queen's who had been discovered in the tunnel. There I sold toothpaste, boot polish, exercise books, fruit drinks, silver and gold paint and lead pencils. I have never fancied myself as a shopkeeper and having no head for figures was unable to compete with sums in marks and pfennigs represented by miserable pieces of paper known as Lagermarks or prisoner of war money. I soon resigned this appointment, though not before I had been able to study the possible uses of silver and gold paint in the making of bogus German uniforms.

After the adventure of the canteen, there came a tremendous outburst of tunnelling in every corner of the castle. Where medieval builders had made deep foundations of stone and filled the spaces between with hard rubble the tunnellers of the twentieth century slowly mined their way. Many tunnels were organised along international and commercial lines, with boards of directors. Floorboards were prised up and ingenious trays of dust laid at the entrance to tunnels to mask the gaping holes below. The chapel, the dentist's surgery, and the sick bay, all had tunnels. Gangs of mole-like beings worked day and night, for nearly every officer in the camp was a man of experience in tunnelling.

In that huge pile upon a cliff with a sheer escarpment on three sides, these tunnels had little prospect of success. I was early convinced that such puny efforts would be of no avail against the mass of rock. Escapers must pit their wits against a frailer element—the Germans themselves. The gap in their defences seemed to lie in the hope that the guards would be deceived by a bold attempt to leave by the front gate in German uniform. But while I brooded on these possibilities I joined the board of an international tunnel. I had no faith in it but it was active and absorbing, and because I still had a sense of being at school I did not wish to be left out of the second eleven.

The "directors" of the tunnel were British, French, Polish and Belgian officers. The entrance was in the Sick Bay or Revier under a bed in one of the wards. The first Polish director of the company was a certain Major Gintel, a diminutive officer of Austrian extraction, with sandy hair, whose smart uniform and spotless black boots were in strong contrast to my ragamuffin clothes, for like many British officers, who had only battledress for uniform, my appearance was decidedly Bohemian. John Hyde-Thomson was in his orange sweater, and we both towered above Major Gintel, slow-marching in his fine boots, as with members of the board we paced the courtyard. At times we were joined by Belgian and French colleagues and an earnest international discussion would begin as to which direction the tunnel should take. As with most international conferences, no decision was reached and it was resolved out of deference to the views of other nations to wait and see.

In spite of this absence of agreement on direction we started on the tunnel with vigour. When the floorboards had been lifted beneath the bed in the Sick Bay, we began to dig under the room used for the distribution of Red Cross parcels to the prisoners. Our knowledge of the geography of the castle was vague. We hoped that having burrowed underneath the Parcels Office, we should be able to sink a vertical shaft for as much as forty or fifty feet. Our plans for digging beyond this point were in confusion and were worthy of Don Quixote himself. Some of my colleagues supposed that travelling at right angles to this shaft, we should emerge from the side of the precipice in a small orchard where, on summer days, the prisoners craning from the windows, watched a girl sunbathing with calculated immodesty.

With the aid of broken knives, forks, door latches and bits of metal picked up or stolen from the Germans, we tried to reach the obviously unattainable. Such activities strengthen the spirit of the prisoner of war. They occupy his mind and body and avoid the tedium which may lead to madness. This renders all escape operations worth while, however remote and harebrained the scheme, unless they conflict with some plan that has a real chance of success.

We tunnelled at night, for in the daytime the German doctor was often in the wards. The tunneller dug for four hours at a stretch, lying flat in a narrow channel in the foundations beneath the Parcels Office. Dressed in old underclothes or pyjamas, grey with cement dust, the man, whose shift it was, worked away with his pathetic piece of metal, lighted by a lamp of fat in a tin-lid. Beside him lay a cardboard Red Cross box into which he carefully scooped the spoil. The shift over, he lifted the boards and peeping into the ward, listened to the breathing of the patients, then gingerly emerged, replacing the mask and filling the crevices of the floorboards with dust. The Red Cross box of debris remained beneath the mask to be collected later. He crept towards an empty bed purposely kept empty for him, by the French doctor in charge of the Sick Bay and slept there till morning when he hastened away before the Germans came to count the patients.

Major Gintel soon became impatient at the slow progress of the tunnel and resigned his place on the board. His successor as Polish representative was Lieutenant Count Feliks Jablonowski of the Polish Horse Artillery, magistrate in Poland and in modern times a solicitor in London. For the next four months we worked each night until the tunnel stretched for twenty feet beneath the Parcels Office.

One aspect of our task was exceptionally difficult and dangerous. It was the disposal of the soil which we took from the tunnel and emptied from the Red Cross boxes into sacks made from coarse German pillow cases. Workers in other tunnels had appropriated every hiding place upon the ground floor of the castle to hide their debris. We were therefore obliged to carry sacks of dusty stones and rubbish up the steep staircase adjoining the Sick Bay every evening. When the courtyard was crowded with prisoners gathering for *Appel* at nine o'clock we would sneak out of the Sick Bay and hustle up the staircase. The results of the previous night of tunnelling were concealed beneath our overcoats and on the top floor we breathlessly emptied the sacks in a darkened loft. This weird and exhausting routine had to be carried out before the German sentries paraded and locked all the doors leading into the courtyard, for a tunneller locked in, perhaps in foreign territory, might have to answer awkward questions.

I was no longer at Colditz when the Germans eventually found the Sick Bay tunnel, after it had been in existence for many months. It was said that a patient in the ward had betrayed it to the Germans.

In that sensitive atmosphere where the minds of prisoners were ready to magnify grievances and suspicions, a great drama shook the camp. The French officers turned on their Jewish companions in misfortune. They requested the Germans to banish the Jews from the quarters which they shared with the Gentiles to a different part of the castle. The Germans were delighted at the success of their propaganda. For days the subject was heatedly discussed by every nation. The camp was divided as to the wisdom and fairness of this anti-Semitism for many of the French officers were suspected of sharing the defeatist sentiments of Vichy. Nevertheless, it was difficult to understand why they should respond to racial discrimination and I never quite fathomed

68

the psychology of this incident. I allied myself with energy to the Jews.

Few of them were keen escapers but the behaviour of their fellow-officers in a Fascist prison-camp seemed to me outrageous. When the Jews held a meeting in their dining-room, I spoke and offered my support against the forces of Vichy. This was a piece of sheer conceit. The small handful of British officers, hoping no doubt to preserve the balance of power, remained aloof and refused to involve themselves in Continental politics. My speech was received with ap-plause, and indeed I benefited materially from my inter-ference. Each week afterwards I attended splendid suppers cooked by an expert Jewish chef from the contents of parcels sent from France.

CHAPTER VI

THE Great Jewish Row subsided slowly and for several days feeling ran high among the nations at Colditz. Some of the French Gentiles were angry with me and two resigned from the Board of the Sick Bay Tunnel in protest at my beha-viour. But the tunnel continued to make progress. I worked two nights a week flat on my stomach with a handkerchief over my mouth to protect my throat from the fine dust. Hyde-Thomson and Jablonowski worked the remainder of the week while others of our company acted as porters of the spoil to the loft above. When several hundredweights of stones and dust had been accumulated on the floor of the loft, part of the ceiling of the room below gave way, burst-ing a pipe and causing a flood among the French Gentiles as they slept.

When I was not working in the tunnel there was time to think of escaping by the front gate dressed as a German soldier. It was first necessary to discover the German system of controlling the entry to the inner courtyard. For many months past the prisoners had formed a "Goon Watch," a continuous observation of enemy activity within the castle. Changing of sentries, movements of the German *Feldwebel* Gephard, know as Mussolini, the state of sobriety of Haupt-mann Priem, the Camp Officer, were noted in a special book. The observer sat high above the courtyard in an alcove looking down upon the gateway through a narrow window. The entry of civilians with carts or wheelbarrows was of special interest and within a minute of their arrival gangs of prisoners had been warned by a messenger to run down and steal their clothes or any implement that might be useful for tunnelling. The watch soon lost its novelty and became a boring duty. It did not escape the notice of the Germans who started a similar system so that each side silently watched the other from the battlements. Yet by this means, much useful information was acquired by the prisoners. For instance, I learned that each person who entered the inner courtyard collected a brass, numbered disc at the guard-house, showed it to the sentry at the gates and returned it to the guard-house on leaving. Once it was delivered to the sentry at the gate it would be possible, in German uniform, to march down the roadway beneath the archways over the moat-bridge to the final gate. One of these discs was acquired during the latter part of June 1941 when an elderly house-painter entered the British quarters. He was succesfully bribed with tobacco by Peter Allan of the Queen's Own Cameron Highlanders, who spoke good German, to leave his disc behind him and inform the guard of its loss. It had already been placed among the communal store of aids to escape.

I had next to find a German uniform for my escape from the castle and suitable attire for making my way four hundred miles to Switzerland. A complete German soldier's uniform might be acquired by corruption over a period of years. But I was impatient to be free. I determined to make a uniform though I had no deftness in my fingers. I bartered a whole month's ration of Red Cross chocolate for an ancient Polish tunic. In a remote sort of way it resembled in length and design that worn by German private soldiers. How could it be rendered field-grey? It was made of smooth, thin cloth of khaki colour. I thought first that I would dye it in a large saucepan on a stove in the passageway leading to the main hall of the British quarters. I had previously dyed battledress trousers with leads taken out of indelible pencils bought at the canteen. The dyeing of clothes in any other colour was, however, unknown to me and I had not by then discovered that the pre-war Dutch Army uniform of blue-green could be converted into passable field-grey.

I lay each night wrestling with my problem. The paint, bought at the canteen for creating a backcloth of trees for the camp theatre provided an amateurish solution. During several evenings I patiently smeared this paint in what I believed was the right shade of field-grey on the surface of the tunic. When the tunic was ready I took it to a Polish tailor who sewed on the left breast pocket cardboard insignia painted in silver. This was also bought at the canteen. The tailor created epaulettes of dark green cloth, each surmounted by numerals in white to indicate an infantry regiment. Next came the marking of a forage cap of German design. This also started as an article of Polish uniform and was plastered with scenery paint and left to dry. I sewed some white piping, denoting German infantry, along the sides and a roughly drawn representation in cardboard of the regular badge of eagle's wings and swastika in front. The trousers which I planned to wear were ordinary R.A.F. trousers, which at night resembled the German uniform trousers of dark grey. For my feet I had bought with Red Cross provisions a splendid pair of jackboots from a Polish orderly which could easily pass for the standard boots of German soldiers.

This hastily contrived disguise could never have passed by daylight. Even if it were possible to get beyond the door of the Inner courtyard and surrender the brass disc, a series of obstacles confronted the escaper. He had first to pass a sentry at the gateway which led into the Outer courtyard and there risk meeting numerous members of the garrison. Then came the clock tower with a sentry standing beneath its vaulted arch and in passing over the moat-bridge there still remained the scrutiny of the sentry at the final gate where a sloping causeway descended into Colditz. I was only too aware of the fancy-dress appearance of my uniform fit only for amateur theatricals. Prisoners, however, develop a blind faith in the most impracticable methods of escape. They underestimate the risks, believing that some kindly Providence will surely aid them.

For me, escaping was still a schoolboy adventure reminiscent of the books of G. A. Henty. I had yet to learn that success can only be achieved by a minute mastery of detail and a study of the mind and methods of the enemy. I had in fact no clear vision of what I should do when I emerged with my brass disc from the courtyard, only some shadowy idea that I would steal a bicycle from a rack in the Outer Courtyard and pedal across the moat-bridge past the sentry at the last gateway. I saw myself dramatically racing down the causeway amid a fusillade of rifle fire from the castle. Self-dramatization is the most dangerous of all defects in an escaper. Once he allows his mind, under the stress of captivity, to wander from the path of common sense, he may not live to tell his tale.

Pat Reid, was a forceful character whose clear thinking during those uncertain months made possible several of the successful escapes from the castle. Powerfully built, he gave an impression of concentrated power enhanced by a quiet, deliberate speaking voice. He made a spectacular escape with three British officers in October 1942 and reached Switzerland where he became assistant military attaché. He was just the man to modify and restrain fanciful plans which might lead to disaster and was not impressed by my "uniform." My fellow-prisoners charitably ignored it, without comment, as befitted a crazily optimistic scheme. The prospects of success were indeed limited. Two Dutch officers disguised as Germans had made an attempt to pass the gate ten days before in broad daylight. They were not equipped with brass discs and were politely escorted by the sentry to the guard-room a few yards away and thence to solitary confinement.

Despite these obvious difficulties and the absurdity of my sham "uniform" I was determined to make the attempt. A hysterical impatience overcame me. I could hardly wait for my disguise to be completed. I decided to make the attempt by night, for I supposed that darkness would conceal some of the defects of my get-up. The manufacture of a weapon now became my chief anxiety. All sentries were equipped with rifles and bayonets, and I aimed to impersonate the humblest rank of N.C.O.—a *Gefreiter* or Lance-Corporal. The making of an imitation rifle was quite beyond my craftsmanship. As the years of war prolonged their captivity, prisoners grew in boldness and resources. In another camp a rifle was perfectly executed in wood, and only detected by the closest scrutiny. But these were the pioneer days of 1941.

I decided to be a *Gefreiter* on some special duty without a rifle, leaving the courtyard to report to Hauptmann Priem. Even for this purpose a bayonet in a scabbard was necessary. An officer of the Royal Tank Regiment carved one with a knife from one of my bed boards and painted it black and silver. His name was O'Hara and his face was the colour of a strawberry. He bore his name of Scarlet with good humour.

Scarlet O'Hara is dead. He died in Canada after the war. I remember him as a shy, unselfish character who delighted in helping, with his skill, those who needed disguises. In such a fraternity the escape of one man may result from the labours of many who never know the triumph of a safe return to liberty. Among the many remarkable men at Colditz were some who sat in the stark rooms day after day helping others to escape. Chances of success were few, even for those who spoke German well. Others who had no such assets found the hours less weary by their devotion to the cause of launching those who had the best chances of getting home. Their sacrifice was not in vain; no less than twenty officers escaped from this strongly guarded castle during the war. Of these eleven were British. The "special punishment camp" had the highest record of successful escapes of any in Nazi Germany.

When Scarlet had finished my bayonet he hung it from a cardboard belt fixed with a buckle of tin foil where the words *"Gott Mit Uns"* around a swastika design adorned the stomachs of German soldiers. For my civilian clothes I had little thought. My plans hardly extended beyond the last gate of the castle. I boiled an R.A.F. tunic in a cauldron darkened by the lead of indelible pencils. This I proposed to wear with a collar and tie and R.A.F. trousers as soon as I had left the camp and could discard my "uniform."

Before my imprisonment at Colditz I had evinced little interest in hats or their manufacture. As I looked at my jacket of indelible blue with civilian buttons I became convinced that I should need a Homburg hat of Teutonic appearance. I lay awake one night when I was not on duty in the tunnel wondering how to make one. My education had been on classical lines. I had never been taught to use my hands, to sew, or engage in household carpentry. I was defeated by the problem. Even Scarlet O'Hara had not attempted such a thing. Ski caps or cloth caps for workmen cut from German Army blankets were the best available.

One day at exercise in the Park, which we took twice a week, I met a Frenchman who had perfected a method of his own which I copied with some success. This method, though decidedly amateurish, did produce a hat of passable design, though I would recommend no one to try it except *in extremis*. To make a hat suitable for German travel; first, take a piece of the thickest blanket available. After measuring the circumference of the head, cut out a brim of appropriate width from the blanket and stiffen it with glue and water. Next attach the brim to a lining of cardboard and, after cutting a piece of blanket suitable size, make the crown and sew to the cardboard lining. Continue by setting the hat like a sort of blancmange in a mould of earth or sand, stiffening with more glue and water. Complete the job by sewing a dark green band around the brim, and sew in place, a suitable feather or small shaving brush, thus attaining a Tyrolean appearance.

The pleasure occasioned by the making of this ridiculous hat was short-lived. Two days after it was made the Germans rushed into the camp on a sudden search of the British quarters for escape materials and captured it under the floorboards of my bed. I had the mortification of seeing a tipsy German officer walking unsteadily in the courtyard with it on top of his uniform hat. I had to be content with a ski cap of indelible blue like my jacket.

There remained the question of maps and compasses and money. I slowly traced in Indian ink the neighbourhood of the Swiss frontier from a stolen map and hid it carefully in a crevice in a wooden partition of the lavatory. A Dutch officer made me a rough identity card for a foreign worker in Germany. I still had the small compass rescued from the Gestapo at Plock, now sewn into the lining of the converted Air Force tunic. The money which I received came from the black market deals with the guards. Lockwood also handed me a mysterious cigar-shaped container about two and a half inches long. He explained, that, to avoid its capture, if I did not get out of the camp, I must carry it in the container inside my rectum. If the container and money were not found I was to return them to him. My experiments with the container caused much hilarity.

Such were the preparations for my escape. I lived in a world of fantasy and of hurried conferences with my tailors and other helpers. My plans absorbed my whole life and influenced every thought and action. At night I dreamed that I was outside the camp and making my way across Germany. By day I made a round of the various hiding places for my painted uniform and civilian clothes in hollow places in the walls, under floorboards, or even in Red Cross boxes in the Sick Bay tunnel, often changing their positions to avoid detection by the Germans.

It was a hot evening early in August 1941 when I went on to the parade ground at nine with a British Army over-coat over my sham uniform. Beneath my overcoat I held my false German cap as I stood among the ranks of British prisoners. Around us at their usual posts beside the locked doors of the different quarters, stood sentries in the darkening courtyard. There were a dozen or so in number, and as I stood there with my heart beating I wondered half-humorously what they would think of their new comrade. The parade continued in its usual fashion, the German officer on duty counting the prisoners of each nation after their numbers had been reported to him by senior officers. Above the castle the sky was clear and still.

The counting done, the order to dismiss was given in a loud German fashion, and the prisoners in a surging mass moved to different doorways to return to their quarters. There was the familiar sound of clogs and laughter as they walked over the cobble stones and up the stone stairs. The sentries began to fall in beside the delousing shed and march away from the courtyard. Someone quickly removed my khaki overcoat from my shoulders. I placed my German cap squarely on my head, stuck out my chest and marched towards the main door.

It was half-open and a German under-officer put his head inside. I spoke to him nervously.

"I have a message to the Kommandant from Haupt-mann Priem."

He took the brass disc from me and let me pass. In the arc lights outside the gate his face seemed pale and anxious. He said nothing but stared at me sharply as I turned on my heel and marched away from the guard-house. My Polish boots rang smartly on the rounded stones of the rampart and my wooden bayonet flapped against my side. On one side was the high wall of the rampart bathed in a fierce light and ahead of me the first archway where the sentry stood in the shadows. I marched quickly, anxious to avoid the lights and reach the bicycles before the alarm was given.

I felt again the sense of being free. It was like a drug which brought an intense pleasure, an exquisite unburdening of the soul. It equalled the moment when Forbes and I had first reached the artillery ground at Thorn and set off under the stars towards the east. I felt that I was acting in a theatre where no audience could hear me. My performance was for my own enjoyment. I smiled to myself and walked on.

When I was close to the first archway, there was a loud shout behind me. The tone of the voice was uncertain.

"Halt!"

There were more shouts from the guard-house as I turned round towards the lights. It was a fatal mistake. I became aware that the scenery paint was glowing under the arc lamps, reflecting in my tunic a shade of pea-green. The painfully designed cap with all its markings was the worst. It shone like a brilliant emerald in the glare. I was a figure of the underworld, a demon king under the spotlights in a Christmas pantomime. I turned and ran panic stricken towards the bicycles.

Heavy footsteps as of a whole army of jackboots pursued me.

"Halt, or I fire!" cried a voice as I reached the archway. It was hopeless. I was not prepared to be shot for having failed so dismally. I turned again and threw up my hands. As I did so the sentry came running from the archway and prodded me in the back with his rifle. In a moment all the inmates of the guard-room were upon me, chattering excitedly and pointing rifles and revolvers. The under-officer in charge had a fit of hysterical rage of particularly Teutonic quality.

"This is an insult to the German Army! You will be shot."

The soldiers around me glowered and dutifully echoed his remarks. A door opened in the Kommandantur and officers came running with drawn revolvers. When the excited crowd around me numbered at least thirty, each man with fire-arm drawn and pointing at me, the tall figure of the Kommandant, Oberst Prawitz, appeared among the crowd which came rapidly to attention. The passion and the threats vanished. Prawitz was dignified and crushing and wore the smartest of uniforms with a decoration hanging from his high collar.

"What impertinence," he said in lofty tones. "Take him away to the cells."

Augustus himself could not have given a more imperial command.

I was led away dejected and forlorn. For a brief moment I had been a self-made hero and now I was only a sad joke in a burlesque German uniform. I was pushed roughly through the door of a solitary-confinement cell and left in utter darkness. I undid my cardboard belt and wooden bayonet and flung them on the floor in rage. It was many hours before I slept.

Next morning a soldier came and brought me *ersatz* coffee. He told me that I was to be court-martialled and shot. I had recovered my spirits and laughed at him angrily. He went away baffled. But the joke was over. I felt tired and worn and, surprisingly enough, extremely liverish. I was no longer afraid but felt foolish. At ten o'clock an under-officer came and ordered me to the Kommandant's headquarters where I stood awkwardly in a long, panelled gallery, closely examined by all the officers of the camp. Their emotions ranged from ridicule to extreme anger as they surveyed my pathetic uniform. A door opened in the gallery and once more the tall Kommandant appeared. He was polite but mocking.

"Stand to attention and salute German fashion," he said. There were bilious spots before my eyes and in my fury I stood awkwardly trying to imitate a German salute.

"A German soldier wouldn't salute like that. Do it again!"

I blushed as the middle-aged German officers laughed obsequiously. I saluted once more. The Kommandant smiled in a superior fashion and returned to his office in silence.

I stood in the gallery for most of the morning under the guard of two sentries. From time to time police officers from Colditz and soldiers were brought in to look at me as if I were a newly captured animal. There was a chorus of Heil Hitler! as they stamped down the gallery. At last the tension relaxed and turned to comic relief. An elderly photographer from the town, dressed in threadbare black clothes arrived with his equipment and bowed in servile fashion to Hauptmann Priem. He looked like a deflated Hindenburg. Slowly he assembled a large Victorian camera on a tripod at the end of the gallery, and photographed me from different angles. I stood there, in the heat of the day, perspiring beneath my dyed jacket which lay under the green tunic. I had reduced all escaping to a ridiculous farce, a music-hall turn. I grew crimson with mortification as the old man doddered about the gallery exchanging feeble jokes with the soldiers. It seemed hours before the comedy was over. Then my German uniform was taken away to be placed in the Kommandant's museum, and I was taken back to the British quarters. There were no more threats of shooting for wearing an enemy uniform. I was to be regarded as an ordinary escaper and would do my time in the cells when there was room in the town gaol.

That evening Hauptmann Priem made the following announcement to the assembled prisoners, which was translated into many languages:

"Gefreiter Neave is to be sent to the Russian Front."

The roar of laughter which greeted this sally was the loudest which I ever heard in the castle. It was friendly towards me but it was not music to my ears.

CHAPTER VII

FOR several weeks after my attempt to escape I remained at the window of the castle sadly watching the approach of autumn. I was still in the British quarters for the number of punishment cells in the castle and the town gaol was insufficient to contain the throng of prisoners under sentence. I waited despondently until there was room for me to undergo my punishment of twenty-eight days' solitary confinement. In early October, when the leaves were blown high over the roofs and began to fall in the courtyard I was sent to the town gaol in Colditz.

At Colditz, prisoners were better treated than at Thorn. There was no damp cavern filled with rotting swedes. My sentence meant a whole month away from the twitter of the camp, surrounded by books in a warm cell. When the order came for me to go to the town, I bundled my favourite books with tobacco, cigarettes and chocolate for many weeks in a blanket. A sentry led me from the courtyard, and as we passed under the gateways along the route of my ill-fated attempt I saw a new white wooden barrier across the road at the final exit. The sentry grinned at me and said,

"They put this here because of you."

I paid no attention to him. I was not interested in the new white barrier. I was concentrating furiously on something I had seen in the wall of the moat-bridge. Looking over it I had seen the moat below, its dry bed filled with heavy stones half-hidden by grass. Down each side of its bank there ran a roughly paved pathway. Steps led from a gap in the wall of the bridge and joined the pathway as it swept steeply down into the moat. Up through the grass of the far bank went the pathway until it vanished near the married quarters of the prison staff at the edge of the park. In the space in the wall of the moat-bridge where the steps began, a little wicket-gate stood half open.

I could hardly contain my excitement. The sentry hearing me crow with delight, turned in surprise. He did not know that I had seen a way of freedom. If I could cross the moat-bridge and reach the Park, escape was possible. On the far side of the moat there was no longer barbed wire, but palings which overlooked the steep slope of trees leading to the Park below. The married quarters, a building on the far bank, represented danger, but once the escaper had climbed the palings he would be sheltered by the trees at night. There remained the ancient stone wall of the Park, twelve feet high and thick with moss.

The white barrier swung open and we began to descend the old causeway to the town. My mind was occupied with the wicket-gate as we marched, unnoticed, through the streets and came to a building like a chapel with a gravel courtyard. The gaoler stood at the door to receive me. He had a pleasant, round red face and white moustache. Fingering his keys he made me open my blanket and looked longingly at my cigarettes and chocolate, then addressed me as "Herr Leutnant." I climbed with him up a stone staircase and entered a cell. Here thieves and drunks had languished

79

in the days of peace. Now, with the manhood of Colditz gone to war, there was room for enemy prisoners.

When the door was locked I climbed on to the bed. I was pleased to be alone. I did not feel caged and helpless as I had done during those terrible hours at Plock. I had almost forgotten the Gestapo. Now I thought only of escape. I tried, but failed, to reach the ledge of the small window cut out in the stonework and look down to the courtyard below. I sank on to the bed and despondently turned my attention to a huge ugly stove. I climbed on to its round top. From there I could feel the surface of the ceiling and the thought came to me that, with a knife, I could cut through the plaster. I thought of hauling myself into the space above and then breaking out through the roof by night, dropping to the courtyard by a rope made from the mattress cover.

As I crouched on the stove, feeling the surface of the ceiling, I failed to hear the footsteps in the passage. The door opened suddenly. The gaoler's jovial face froze as, for a moment, he must have thought the cell was empty. Then he saw me squatting disconsolately above him. He laughed loudly, jangling enormous keys.

"So soon, Herr Leutnant! You must stay with us a few days longer."

Next day I was moved to a cell on the ground-floor where the twenty-eight days passed agreeably. I had enough cigarettes for months and lay on my bed smoking and reading save for an hour's exercise in the courtyard. In my cell I was far from war. The mighty events of 1941 disturbed me not at all. Tobruk and Pearl Harbor never interrupted my secluded peace. I was withdrawn from the world fancying myself in a cottage in the Lake District, sometimes with Jane Eyre, sometimes with the Duchess of Wrexe. When I was taken from the gaol and marched back to the castle I saw once more the little wicket gate in the wall of the moat-bridge. At nights it appeared in my dreams as the gateway to the land beyond the Blue Mountains.

As autumn gave way to winter of that monotonous year I joined in the plans of the British prisoners to produce a variety show in the camp theatre.

The camp theatre was a great room on the second floor of the building adjoining the gates of the inner courtyard. In this building senior officers of the Allied Nations were quartered. Here lived a French General, a Polish Admiral, and a Polish General with senior British officers. Connecting this building with the guard-house was the mysterious Bridge of Sighs. What lay behind those tiny dusty windows above the gateway? Was there a passageway leading to the attic on the upper floor of the guard-house? At either end of the bridge the rooms which led to it were locked and barred and doors bricked up. Roaming like inquisitive children around some mysterious mansion in the hours of daylight, we came excitedly upon the secret. There was a passageway. *The way to it lay under the floor of the theatre where a rough dais was raised to form a stage.*

The prospectors in this new territory were led by Pat Reid and "Hank" Wardle, M.C., a Canadian in the R.A.F., who first discovered the magic entrance. "Hank" was a very tall man of immense physical strength. He was of quiet disposition but immensely shrewd and, though he spoke little, his judgment in matters of escaping was excellent. He had already made one attempt to escape from Spangenburg. Pat Reid and he reached Switzerland in October 1942. Neither "Hank" nor I could have foreseen at this time that eighteen months later I should be his Best Man at his wedding in England!

Beneath the stage the searchers found space enough to crawl and slowly sawed away the floorboards with stolen implements, making a square hole in the ceiling of the passage below. To disguise this hole Reid made an ingenious mask known as "Shovewood." Then, with the usual rope of mattress covers tied to one of the supports of the stage, he climbed down into the sealed passage. Facing him was a locked door leading to the gate-bridge. He picked the lock and, walking softly in slippered feet through the musty air, he came to a further door on the far side of the bridge. It opened without difficulty, revealing steps into an attic above the guard-house. On the floor beneath was the German Officers' Mess and up the stairs into this gloomy place came the hoarse laughter of Hauptmann Priem and the tinkle of glasses.

Pat Reid proposed that teams of two, one British and one Dutch officer, should attempt to escape disguised as German officers. He selected John Hyde-Thomson and myself and we both set to work to make the uniforms. My friends were not enthusiastic. The failure of other attempts had disheartened them. They did not believe that even in a German uniform would it be possible to get past the guardroom, and there were disheartening though friendly comments.

"It will only alert the Goons."

"You are being rather selfish."

"I can't think why they allow you to go."

"My dear chap, I knew about the wicket gate months ago."

I learned at Colditz that the escaper must have absolute confidence in his success. He must never be discouraged by the gloom of his companions or he is lost. He must above all calmly choose the right moment to attack. It seemed to me that if two men in German officers' uniforms were to descend the stairs from the attic and emerge from the guard-house door through the passage which the door of the actual guard-room opened, their appearance would not be questioned by the sentry outside. What more natural than that two officers, after visiting the mess above, should appear from the guard-room door walking towards the Kommandantur? From the moment that the passage was discovered, I concentrated every thought on how to fool the sentry who was posted outside the guard-room. If the man were cold and bored with duty on a winter's night, would his numbed brain suspect two officers coming from his own guard-house?

*　　*　　*

A pantomime produced by British officers in a prison camp is always pathetic. No amount of ingenuity exercised by stage managers and costume makers can conceal its futility. Senior officers with large moustaches appear half-naked as chorus girls in brassieres and ballet skirts of paper. Good-looking officers appear as leading ladies and rougher customers as red-nosed comedians. Although such an occupation keeps the prisoners from brooding on their fate, the actual performances are ghastly. On only one occasion do I remember seeing any real acting, that was in a sensitive performance of Journey's End at Spangenburg produced by Michael Langham of the Black Watch.

During preparations for the guard-house escape, I was able to write and produce a section of the pantomime, which was a three-act sketch entitled "The Mystery of Wombat

College." The principal character in this episode was Dr. Calomel, an unpleasant headmaster. The remainder of the inhabitants of the college, particularly the masters, were persons of bad character. It is difficult to say whether, in a normal atmosphere, this wretched little piece would be regarded as funny, but it was an uproarious success in the all-male atmosphere of Oflag IVc. The only disapproval came from the French officers who were of the opinion that English public school life was a subject lacking in real humour. I watched them smile indulgently during the rehearsals at my lack of taste.

I decided to play the part of Dr. Calomel myself. I created the part of a leering headmaster with heavy black brows resembling Groucho Marx. My costume consisted of a gown and a mortar-board made of black paper, and a pair of steel-rimmed spectacles. During the rehearsals the obscenity of the dialogue and the cynicism of the performance caused an entirely justifiable protest from the Chaplains. One of them made the biting comment that a play which appeared to be written for Old Etonians, was not suited to an international prison camp!

When the rehearsals began at the end of November, under the direction of Teddy Barton of the R.A.S.C., the discovery of the way to the guard-house had just been made. I took no part in the lock-picking or the carpentry involved in making a hole in the ceiling, as I was busy with the production of my sketch. One afternoon while I was rehearsing a scene in which Dr. Calomel was tearfully expelling the younger son of a Duke, I heard muffled thuds beneath the stage. The figure of Pat Reid and his assistant "Hank" Wardle, appeared from below covered in dust and plaster. They had good news of the escape route. In the excitement I forgot my part. Dr. Calomel, blackmailed by one of his pupils, was due to pace the stage gloomily intoning:

O mihi praeteritos referat si Jupiter annos!

As the weeks passed in rehearsal, I searched for a new and more authentic German uniform. My first and most valuable acquisition was a long, green uniform overcoat of an officer of the Netherlands Home Army. There were in the camp upwards of sixty officers of the Dutch Forces, who, rather than take an oath of allegiance to Hitler, had resolved to spend the war in captivity. All of them were men of high character who spoke good English and German. Most of the officers were of the Netherlands East Indies Army, whose uniform was a shade of jungle green and unsuitable for my purpose. The pre-war Home Army, however, had blue-green uniforms, whose colour could easily pass at night for field grey.

The Dutch and the British had early come to an agreement upon escape matters. Since the Dutch officers spoke German they were allowed to take part in British schemes and share the store of aids to escape. They also volunteered to hand over pieces of their uniform for the escape from the guard-house. The final plan agreed on envisaged the escape of two parties of bogus German officers at an interval of twenty-four hours. The first party would consist of Lieutenant Toni Luteyn of the Netherlands East Indies Army and myself. The second would consist of John Hyde-Thomson and Lieutenant Donkers of the Netherlands East Indies Army.

A bogus German uniform had to be most carefully hidden, for the enemy made constant searches of the room where I slept and of all my belongings. I was obliged to keep the precious Dutch overcoat rolled in some sacking under the floorboards beneath a "mask." If this hiding place were suspected another would have to be found.

Such was the talent in the camp that I had no difficulty in discovering officers who could convert the Dutch material into a very passable German officer's overcoat. The epaulettes, normally of woven silver braid, were made from thick linoleum cut from the floor of the bathroom, painted silver and sewn to the shoulders.

I had decided to promote myself to the rank of Oberleutnant and to take on the identity of an infantry officer named Schwartz. It was therefore necessary to provide small gold stars to denote that rank. These were fashioned from wood, cut with a penknife by Scarlet O'Hara and painted gold. Although the Germans, after several discoveries of imitation uniforms, stopped supplies of silver and gold paint to the canteen, a quantity had been saved and carefully stored. The epaulettes were finished with a gold numeral to denote an infantry regiment. There remained only the collar of the overcoat and the buttons. A dark green collar

84

was cut from green baize material. The buttons were of lead from lavatory piping poured into skilful moulds made by the Dutch. My belt on this occasion was of cardboard painted brown from a box of water colours, and with a fine imitation revolver holster of cardboard filled with newspaper. My disguise was nearly complete.

Much of this faithful work was done for me by Squadron Leader Brian Paddon, D.S.O., D.F.C. Paddon was the most ingenious mind among escapers of my experience. He eclipsed even Scarlet O'Hara in the picking of locks and making of keys. Obsessed by such technicalities, he amassed a vast hoard of implements many of which he absent-mindedly carried in his pockets. At nightfall he could be seen making the rounds of his private hiding-places or testing the strength of ancient locks. His long face bore an expression of morose determination as he haunted the more mysterious corners of the castle. His persevering nature was rewarded by a brilliantly successful exploit. He was returned to Stalag XXa to stand his court-martial for insulting the German *Feldwebel* who had thrown Forbes and myself into the dungeons at the end of our escape in Poland. As the court was due to assemble, Paddon broke out of his cell and after many adventures reached the safety of neutral Sweden in 1942.

Among the many gadgets and contrivances provided by the fanatical Paddon was a German officer's uniform cap. In the army of the Third Reich an officer's cap had a black shiny peak resembling that of a chauffeur. Towards the beginning of December, I made a remarkable discovery concerning my own service dress uniform cap which had been sent to me by my parents in a parcel. I stripped it of khaki material and discovered to my astonishment that underneath, it had a bright black shiny peak. Paddon bent the brim and sides of the cap so that it stood high above the peak, and covered the whole with Dutch uniform material. The principal badge, a design of leaves in silver with a roundel in white and red in the centre, he cut from a piece of linoleum. The familiar eagle's wings and swastika design, also in linoleum, were sewn above. He finished this masterpiece by sewing white piping on the edge of the brim. With such a uniform I could face the arc lights once more with confidence.

Through that icy December, I rehearsed the part of Dr. Calomel by day and collected the parts of my uniform by night. On several occasions precious pieces met with disaster. Epaulettes of linoleum and badges carelessly left about were found and confiscated. Often tragedies came thick and fast. John Hyde-Thomson sat on his German hat crushing the carefully poised brim; there was a shortage of lead piping from the lavatories; the prisoners were banned from the theatre for several days for stealing a workman's coat.

Undeterred, we hastened our preparations in a running fight with the searching guards.

Toni Luteyn, my Dutch companion, was playing the drums in the camp orchestra which accompanied the musical part of "Ballet Nonsense." Since we were both occupied in the theatre we were able to transfer our disguises in Red Cross boxes underneath the stage. I rehearsed the coarse absurdities of Wombat College, wondering how long it would be before the Germans decided to look beneath the stage.

It was bitterly cold and snow lay on the ground for many days as the time for the opening of the pantomime drew near. I had hoped to combine my escape with my appearance in the part of Dr. Calomel. This was a situation which appealed not only to my sense of humour, but it had its merits as a plan to deceive the Germans. The programme opened with a chorus of heavy masculine beauties crashing about the stage followed by "The Mystery of Wombat College." Then came a number of individual acts and a musical scene nostalgically set in a London pub. This was the grand finale with all performers singing the praises of the "Rose and Crown." If officers from the camp staff were present at the final performance a day or two before Christmas, Luteyn and I would be able to crawl under the stage before the finale. Then, under cover of deafening music above, we would descend to the passageway by the sheet rope carrying our uniforms in boxes. We would then remove our theatre costumes and dress ourselves as German officers. The thought of disappearing under the stage in the costume of Dr. Calomel and reappearing in German uniform outside the guard-house delighted me.

This ambitious, if sensational, plan proved impossible. When the curtain was due to rise at the beginning of the show, which was announced for three nightly performances, our German uniforms were not complete. We had suffered severe losses of material and our papers as foreign workers were unfinished. These documents were vital to success. We had planned to remove the German uniform overcoats and caps when we were outside the Park walls and bury them in the woods. Underneath the overcoats we were to be disguised as Dutch workers for the journey through enemy territory.

The postponement of the attempt to escape from the guard-house until after Christmas, enabled me to put finishing touches to "The Mystery of Wombat College." I added a new scene in which Dr. Calomel addressed his pupils at the outbreak of the war in a manner which bore an obvious resemblance to Hitler. At each performance embarrassed German clerks and interpreters took notes of any political allusions. The roar of applause on the last night when Dr. Calomel lifted his hand three times in salute, shouting imprecations at the pupils in Latin, resulted in a sly reprimand from Hauptmann Priem.

*   *   *

The pantomime was over, and in the next week before Christmas snow fell thickly in the courtyard. In the British quarters, we ate plum pudding and drank a highly alcoholic brew distilled from dried fruits upon the kitchen stove. Quantities of this mixture had been stored for the occasion and there was great hilarity among the prisoners on Christmas Eve. Some danced, some vomited, some fell unconscious for hours. In the midst of the orgy the door opened and a German officer entered to wish us a German Christmas. The laughter ceased abruptly and there was a silence so deliberate and terrible, that it struck the German like a blow in the face. He looked blankly about him, saluted, and disconsolately withdrew.

The prisoners walked unsteadily into the courtyard and paraded for *Appel* in the snow. From somewhere beyond the gates came the sound of German voices singing Christmas hymns and in the courtyard the strains of "Auld Lang Syne." By a prearranged plan, the prisoners shuffled their feet within the ranks so that an immense "V" sign was formed in the snow. When the parade was over we ran up

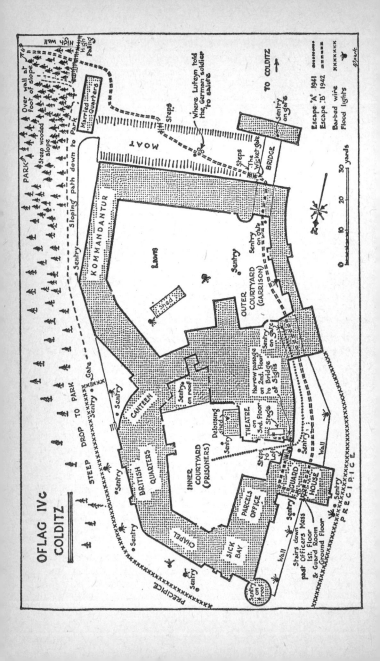

OFLAG IVc
COLDITZ

PARK

Over wall at foot of slope

High Wall

High Paling

Steep wooded slope

Married Quarters

Sloping path down to Park

Steps

Where Luteyn told the German soldier to salute

MOAT

Steps

The Wicket Gate

BRIDGE

Sentry on gate

TO COLDITZ

Escape 'A' 1941
Escape 'B' 1942
Barbed wire
Flood lights

0   10   20   30 yards

KOMMANDANTUR

Lawn

Shed

OUTER COURTYARD (GARRISON)

Sentry on gate

Sentry on gate

Sentry

STEEP DROP TO PARK

Gate

Sentry

Sentry

Sentry

CANTEEN

Sentry on roof

BRITISH QUARTERS

Narrow passage on 2nd. Floor to Bridge of Sighs

Sentry on gate

Delousing shed

THEATRE on 3rd. Floor

1st. Stage

INNER COURTYARD (PRISONERS)

Steps to loft

Sentry

Sentry

Wall

PARCELS OFFICE

GUARD HOUSE

Sentry

PRECIPICE

CHAPEL

SICK BAY

Stairs down past Officers Mess 1st. Floor & Guard Room on Ground Floor

Sentry

Sentry

Sentry

Sentry

Sentry

Sentry

Wall

Sentry on roof

PRECIPICE

to our quarters to look down on the courtyard. A small group of Germans were standing motionless, looking balefully at the ground before them. The great "V" sign was there in the snow, a symbol of hope and defiance.

On the morning of 5th January, 1942, Luteyn and I were ready to escape. We held a conference with Pat Reid and Hank Wardle and decided to try immediately after the nine o'clock *Appel* that evening. Our compasses, maps and a small bundle of notes were ready for hiding inside our bodies. The uniforms were now intact beneath the stage and our civilian clothes had so far escaped detection in their "hide." In a moment of supreme confidence, I collected the addresses of relatives of my companions. Then flushed and excited, I lay down to sleep throughout the afternoon and early evening.

A few minutes before nine I went down to the courtyard, when the snow was falling lightly. The turrets cast long shadows in the light of the moon and the steep walls enfolded me for what I believed to be the last time. There was once more the eternal sound of hundreds of men taking their meagre exercise in clogs. I stood waiting for the *Appel*, eyeing the Dutch contingent where Luteyn was waiting ready to join me. We wore cardboard leggings painted with black polish. I wore my usual combination of battledress and sweater, and my Army boots, being brown, were also darkened with black polish. Underneath I had my "civilian clothes" with a pair of R.A.F. trousers. I had an overpowering sense that this was my last evening in the castle. The certainty grew with every minute, making me composed and determined.

There was a sharp order of dismissal and mingling with the dispersing prisoners, Pat Reid, "Hank" Wardle, Luteyn and I hurried quickly into the senior officers' quarters. In the darkness of the theatre, we felt our way beneath the stage, then carefully prised up the loose floorboards. Pat Reid lifted the trap called "Shovewood" which, on its underside was whitewashed, disguising the hole in the ceiling of the passage below. I could see the strong, determined lines on his face as he worked in the glow of a cigarette-lighter. The trap removed, the mattress-cover rope was let down through the hole in the ceiling. Cautiously we climbed down, holding the boxes of uniforms, and landed with soft bumps on the floor of the passage.

The bright lights from the courtyard shone through the cobwebbed windows in the outer wall of the passage. Treading softly in our socks, we reached the door of the gate-bridge. Pat Reid, shining his lighter on the lock, swiftly picked it. It opened without a sound for he had oiled the hinges earlier in the week. We were in the half-light of a narrow corridor. We walked quietly across it and stopped at the door that led to the guard-house.

The German uniform overcoats were unpacked in silence and we put them over our workmen's clothes, leaving our battledress in the boxes. As we pulled on our boots there was no sound except the grating of Pat Reid's wire searching in the lock. A minute passed, and suddenly came fear and exasperation. The door would not open. Beneath our feet we could hear the creaking of the gates and the voices of sentries changing guard. We stood motionless, fully dressed as German officers, and waited with pounding hearts. Pat Reid spoke in a hoarse whisper,

"I'm afraid I can't get it open!"

He continued turning the wire in the lock. I could hear the wire rasping against the rusty metal as he tried again and again to open it. Ten minutes passed in terrible suspense. Through the cobwebbed window I could see the snow falling. I folded my arms and waited. Suddenly there was the noise of old hinges creaking. A quick snap and the door swung open, showing us the dim interior of the attic.

"Good luck," said Pat Reid, and shook hands.

We waited till the door was locked behind us and we could no longer hear his muffled steps. Then we crept carefully to the top of stone spiral stairs at an open door on the other side of the attic. A wireless in the guard-room on the ground floor was playing organ music. It was the moment to go down, for the music was loud. We walked quickly down the first flight of stairs, past the door of the officers' mess on the first floor where a light showed beneath. We waited, then stepped confidently down through darkness, into the passage beside the guard-room. The guard-room door was half-open, and I caught a glimpse of German uniforms inside, as we marched smartly into the blinding whiteness of the snow under the arc lights.

The testing time had come. I strode through the snow trying to look like a Prussian. There stood the sentry, the fallen snow covering his cap and shoulders, stamping his feet, just as I had pictured him. He saluted promptly, but he stared at us, and as our backs were turned I felt him watching. We walked on beneath the first archway and passed the second sentry without incident. Then, between the first and second archways, two under-officers talking loudly came from the Kommandantur. They began to march behind us. I felt Luteyn grow tense beside me. I clasped my hands behind my back with an air of uncon-cern. I might have been casually pacing an English parade ground. In a moment of excitement I had forgotten my part. "March with your hands at your sides, you bloody fool," came a fierce sharp whisper from my companion.

Again I saw the bicycles near the clock tower. Could they be ridden fast in this thick snow? We passed beneath the tower, saluted by the sentry, and came to the fateful wicket-gate. As Luteyn opened it I watched the under-officers, their heads bowed to the driving snow, march on across the moat bridge. Down we went into the moat, stumbling and slip-ping, until we reached its bed. A soldier came towards us from the married quarters. He reached us, stopped and stared deliberately. I hesitated for a moment ready to run, but Luteyn turned on him quickly and in faultless German said crossly, "Why do you not salute?"

The soldier gaped. He saluted still looking doubtful and began to walk up the side of the moat towards the wicket-gate. We did not look back but hastened up to the path on the far side, and, passing the married quarters, came to the high oak paling which bordered the pathway above the park. We were still within the faint glare of searchlights. Every moment that we stayed on the pathway was dan-gerous. Lifting ourselves quickly over the paling, we landed in thick snow among the tangle of trees. My cardboard belt was torn and broken and with it into the darkness vanished the holster.

Groping among the trees we struggled through frozen leaves down the steep bank and made for the outer stone wall. It was five minutes before we were at the bottom of the slope. Helped by Luteyn, I found a foothold in the stones of the wall and sat astride the coping. The wall, descending steeply with the tree-covered slope, was shrouded in snow and ice. Each time that I tried to pull Luteyn on top, I lost my foothold and slid backwards through the steep angle of the wall. Then with numbed hands, I caught him beneath the armpits and, after great efforts, hoisted him up beside me. For a minute we sat breathless in the cold air clinging to the coping, and then jumped a distance of twelve feet. We fell heavily on the hard ground in the woods outside the castle grounds. I was bruised and shaken and frightened. I stood leaning against a tree looking at Luteyn. Another minute passed in the falling snow.

"Let's go," I said, and we began to climb towards the east seeking the direction of Leisnig, a small town six miles away.

CHAPTER VIII

At ten o'clock the snow was falling less thickly and the moon showed us a way through the trees as we continued to climb towards the road to Leisnig. Beyond the trees we stumbled over frozen fields with hearts uplifted. The head-lights of a car, yellow in the bright moonlight, turned in our direction. We lay flat in the snowdrifts till the lights swung towards the east. As we felt the hard surface of the road, I turned up the collar of my dark blue jacket against the cold. I had left the warm green overcoat behind me buried with the rest of the uniform beneath a pile of leaves and snow. The blue jacket was made from an officer's uniform of the Chasseurs Alpins. Shorn of silver galons and badges it became a rough workman's coat of serviceable cloth. I was given it by a Jewish officer, Capitaine Boris, who sacrificed his smart uniform for my escape. Boris was an elderly business man, a reserve officer in the Chasseur Alpins and a great patriot. Such was the splendid comradeship of Colditz and one of the results of my interference in the Jewish Row.

On my head I wore a ski cap made of blanket and my Royal Air Force trousers were now turned down over my Army boots. From this moment Luteyn and I were Dutch electrical workers with papers permitting us to change our place of occupation from Leipzig to Ulm in South-Western Germany. Leipzig was twenty-two miles from the castle. We planned to reach it by walking the six miles to Leisnig, and there to take an early workman's train. Foreign workers, it was said, were numerous in Leipzig and some were to be transferred to the south.

We had no papers for the journey to Leipzig. Success depended on our safe arrival at the main station for the south. Pausing a while beside the road, we recovered money, maps and papers from the containers concealed in our bodies and then trudged smartly along the road. After two hours we passed a row of cottages close to Leisnig and came to what appeared to be a barracks. A faint light shone from the entrance gate and in the moonlight we saw a sentry. We stopped, turned from the road, and floundered through deep snow towards a belt of trees on higher ground. We stood there, sheltering among the trees against the sharp winds of the night. The ingenious Dutch officers in Colditz had acquired by bribery a timetable of the trains from Leisnig to Leipzig. We therefore knew that the first workmen's train was due to start at five o'clock. Three hours passed. It was too cold to talk. We waited silently for the train, looking towards the town and listening to the sound of shunting on the railway.

There was not a stir in all that crystal stillness as we climbed down the slope, broke through a hedge, and came back to the road. The road descended into a valley and walking boldly down the main street to the station we passed an early morning traveller and exchanged greetings. There was peace in the little town with its spires and snow-covered roof-tops. I thought of an illustration to the children's tale, *The Tailor of Gloucester* where a lone figure walks through the sleeping city. We had half an hour to wait. There was no one at the station so we walked away to the outskirts of the town unnoticed.

When the train was due we came slowly back to the entrance of the station where a small group of German working people had collected at the gate. As is the custom, the travellers were not allowed on the platform until the train was due to start. We stood silently aside from the others sheltering from the cold beside a wooden hut. When it was nearly five o'clock the doors opened, and the crowd surged forward to the ticket office. We followed in their wake and Luteyn, who spoke the best German, stopped at the *guichet* and bought two workmen's tickets to Leipzig. I followed him on to the platform where we stood apart from the others, men and women carrying small baskets or bags of tools.

The orange front light of an engine appeared. It was a scene of true romance. Here were we, escaped enemy prisoners of war, standing on the platform of the little station, mingling with ordinary people travelling to their daily work. The train, puffing with determination through the snow, halted and we climbed into a wooden carriage.

We were herded together in the semi-darkness of air-raid precautions. The warmth inside the carriage covered the windows with moisture so that I could hardly see the dawn. I bowed my head and dozed beside an old, and evil-smelling market-woman. Suddenly I was awakened by a sharp kick on my shins and looked up in fear. I met the half-smiling eyes of Luteyn. He sat hunched in a short tight overcoat, his ski cap on one side. Then I realised that I must have been talking English in my sleep. No one had noticed or even listened to my murmurs. I watched the thin, strained faces of the working-men as they dozed shoulder to shoulder, and saw the dawn slowly appear through the sweaty windows.

I felt ashamed that Luteyn was more alert and awake. He was strongly-built with humorous grey eyes and long dark hair. He was a strong and buoyant character whose life was spent in laughter and good fellowship. Yet he had a Dutch quality of thoroughness which made him a great escaper. He had staying power and resourcefulness and his great advantage lay in his superior knowledge of Germany and its language, so that he could take each fence with boldness and aplomb. He had a gay, attractive manner of speaking which disarmed the enemy and saved us both in the many dangerous situations which were to follow. For my part, rebellious by temperament though I was, I found him easy to work with and we seldom argued with each other.

At six o'clock we drew in to the great station of Leipzig. The travellers, woken by shrill whistles, began to yawn and swear in low exhausted voices. We looked around us and followed the crowd towards a barrier where we gave up our tickets. There came upon me a sense of alarm and bewilderment. It was twenty months since I had seen the outside world, except for my adventures in the wild desolate country of Poland. Here, among the silent crowds of people moving in the dim light of the station, I was aghast at my helplessness. I felt like a peasant come for the first time to a city, unable to comprehend the paraphernalia of civilisation.

We wandered timidly round the station watching the indicators for a train to Ulm and found that no train left until 10.30 in the evening. It slowly dawned on us that we must stay in Leipzig with nowhere to shelter or sleep for many hours. We tried to find refreshment. Entering a tea-room we ordered coffee, supplied with a small envelope of saccharine. This was all we could obtain, for every other article of food required coupons. The coffee warmed us as we looked shyly at each other, smiling a little, and not daring to speak in any language. After paying for our coffee we wandered to a waiting-room crowded with travellers, mostly poor, who sat among their luggage and children, silent and obedient. I looked at these victims of Hitler's war and felt a great pity. The hopelessness in their faces brought a stark realisation of suffering. We had heard rumours of their plight in the camp, they were now confirmed beyond our belief. Musing I took from my pocket a huge bar of Red Cross chocolate and began to eat.

A young woman with fierce hysterical eyes, gazed at the chocolate as if she had seen a ghost. I stared back at her uncomprehending. She spoke to an old woman beside her and they looked at me in anger. Immediately the crowd near us began to talk in threatening whispers. I heard the word *tchokalade* many times. Luteyn turned to me and frowned angrily. Slowly realising the danger of my position, I put the chocolate back in my pocket. I had committed a terrible blunder. Chocolate had been unknown to working Germans for many months. Goering himself may well have tasted little. We British prisoners were well supplied. To sit eating this forbidden delicacy in the waiting-room of a great station made one not only an object of envy but of deep suspicion. We rose awkwardly and walked out of the waiting-room into the town.

Leipzig at nine in the morning on January the 6th, 1942. The snow was cleared from the streets and there was a distant hum of traffic in the sunshine. Military vehicles sped by us filled with hard-looking men in steel helmets who ignored the civilians. The sidewalks were a mass of field-grey and the mauve-blue of the Luftwaffe. We stared into the shop windows, gazing like children at expensive dresses and furs. Around us stiff, bourgeois, young men in uniform tapped their smart black boots on the pavement, as they stood before the shops. Blonde girls, in short skirts, looked up at the soldiers with fiercely possessive blue eyes and clutched them tightly.

We entered a big emporium and moved among bright lights and dance music and tinsel finery. We watched the people strolling by the counters. The Germans were young, confident and hopeful and we, mere beggars with a few bars of precious chocolate, had only our own high courage between us and the enemy on every side. Only a few sad civilians of an older generation, shabby and worn, crept among the counters like wraiths. The Nazi Revolution of Destruction was at hand.

We were bitterly disappointed to see no sign of bombing, yet the civilians looked hungry and unhappy. We threaded our way through the crowd and came to a square of gardens where a few old men and women walked in the sunshine with their dachshunds. I could read memories in their worn faces and their hatred of Hitler's New Order. I sat beside Luteyn on a seat watching their slow, hopeless perambulation among the snowbound flower beds and shrubs. For me the months of imprisonment were gone and past. I was a detached spectator watching Life go by. New sights and sounds, fresh and clear, came to me after the darkness of prison. Elderly business men and lawyers with briefcases under their arms marched past muttering sombrely to each other. A girl left the procession of Life and sat beside me.

She was young and blonde and plainly of the working class. She looked at me sharply as she sat on the wooden seat. She wore a torn old overcoat and her short tight skirt was above her bare knees. She looked down at her shoes with *ersatz* wooden heels and kicked at a heap of snow. Her mouth was set in a hard determined line. I struggled to look at her calmly but with an inwardly beating heart. Her prominent blue eyes had ruthlessness.

"Good morning," she said.

I dared not answer or risk conversation. She pouted. "You are unsociable, my friend."

I turned to see Luteyn had already risen from the seat and was walking slowly away. I followed him in dismay and embarrassment and, for a moment, turned towards the girl. She was looking hard at us. I felt her blue eyes watching, deep with suspicion and annoyance. We hurried away and wandered among the side streets of Leipzig till it was noon.

A cinema in enemy territory is a fine hiding place for the fugitive. After a lunch of *ersatz* coffee we came to a cheap stuffy cinema at the bottom of an arcade. Luteyn bought the tickets. Our small stock of German marks was enough for only the cheapest seats. We stood, obediently waiting for the performance, regimented by a commissionaire. In a few minutes, we took our seat among German soldiers and sailors and their girls and waited for the curtain, and, as the lights went out, a tall young German officer came in alone and sat next to me.

We saw first on the programme a news-film of events in Libya. Rommel, standing beside a staff car in the desert, talking decisively; then excellent shots of panzers in action and a British plane being shot down. Close ups followed of a British pilot taken prisoner by the Germans and waving encouragement to his friends still fighting in the air. In my excitement I clutched the seat in front of me and was rewarded by the occupant turning round with a harsh whisper of protest.

The feelings of a prisoner who for many months has been shut out from the war and accustomed only to the crudest enemy propaganda, are hard to describe. I could have wept from joy. At least the war was not yet lost. In the next part of the news-film there came a most shattering revelation. The scene was set in a Russian winter. Up a long snow-bound hill German soldiers struggled against the blizzard, dragging guns and vehicles. There were photographs of frozen bodies and men's limbs swollen to unrecognisable size with frost-bite. If Goebbels wanted to impress the Germans with the sufferings of their troops to inspire them to greater sacrifices at home, he hid no detail of their hardships.

There was a shocked silence when the news-film came to an end. The lights went up in the shabby hall while martial music played from a cracked loudspeaker. Young men and girls chanted Nazi songs and around us their clear voices sounded in perfect harmony. Only the old people were glum and quiet. The music changed to

"We are marching against England!"

For a moment I caught my companion's eye and, with a faint grin on our faces, Luteyn and I sang loudly with the rest.

The remainder of the programme was a film set in early nineteenth-century Germany. The heroine, a hard-faced simpering creature, was surrounded by heavy Prussian admirers. The scene which won the most applause was that in which the witty girl took refuge in an earth closet at the bottom of the garden to repel their advances. It was a hut with two heart-shaped holes cut in the door to which she pointed knowingly as she entered. The Germans roared without restraint and we, unimpressed by their lavatory humour, were constrained to do the same for fear of detection.

In the early afternoon the snow began to fall again and the streets of Leipzig seemed full of foreboding for us. A policeman watched us, and followed stealthily until we evaded him among dark alleyways. Working our way back towards the big shops and the crowds, we came to another cinema where there was an atmosphere of plush warmth, antiseptic, and wurlitzer music. We saw the same news-film again as we sat high in the gallery among more German troops on leave. Then came a royal fanfare of trumpets and Hermann Goering appeared on the screen appealing for higher output for the war. He wore the grey uniform in which I was later to see him in his cell at Nuremberg, but with a lavish display of decorations. His throaty voice rasped out propaganda to an audience which remained quiet if respectful. When his vulgar performance had lasted ten minutes there came shots of goose-stepping battalions of Nazis and someone struck up the *Horst Wessel Lied*. But the singing was cheerless and half-hearted.

From the cinema we walked again into the blackout of the city. The moon had not yet risen and only the soft whiteness of the snow guided us through public gardens to the main station. Often at corners of the streets we caught the faint reflection of a policeman's polished helmet and edged away among the crowds or dodged the trams to cross the street.

We came again to the station waiting-room and sat there tired and cold and anxious. The numerous passengers in the waiting-room, many poor and infirm, assembled for the night trains. Then came the men in uniform, elbowing all the civilians aside. I watched them closely. The bullying S.S. men, the clod-like infantrymen, and the pale, and spectacled administrative clerks. All in uniform, they tramped over the gloomy station like locusts, demanding refreshment or newspapers or anything they wanted. Such is total war.

Luteyn bought the tickets to Ulm. We had decided to change there and, if all went well, to take tickets to the Swiss frontier. At the barrier of the platform for the train to the south, military police stood to check the soldiers but there seemed no control of civilians. We waited beside the train before it started, preferring to find standing room than risk conversation in a compartment. As it began to move we climbed the steps of a carriage and stood in the corridor.

The compartment opposite was occupied by a single figure in the uniform of the S.S. I could see the man as we stood outside, a great ape-like person with a heavy jaw. His uniform was new and spotless and he crossed his legs which were in fine black boots as he read a newspaper with screaming red and black headlines. I caught only the word "Rommel." So that he should not watch us, we moved into the shadow at the end of the corridor and looked into the darkness where only a few pin-points of light showed the effective blackout of the city. The train jolted over the points and gathered speed with piercing whistles. Above its rattle I heard the door of the compartment open, and turning my head saw the big S.S. man standing in the doorway. His hands were on each side of the entrance door and he spoke to us in a soft voice.

"Are you Jews?"

"Certainly not. We are Dutch," replied Luteyn.

"Good. Come in and sit here. This compartment was reserved, but my friends are not coming."

We took our seats beside the big man who spoke very slowly to us, using simple phrases. His friendliness alarmed me.

"Where are you travelling?"

"To Ulm."

"Why?"

"We are Dutch electrical workers transferred there from Leipzig."

Luteyn was doing the talking. He had his genuine Dutch passport ready to produce in an emergency. Then the man turned to me and his stupid eyes examined my face, searching for something he did not understand.

"You are Dutch, too?"

"Yes."

"How are things in Holland?"

"We have not been there for some months. We have been in Leipzig since the summer."

It was Luteyn who spoke. The S.S. man turned to me.

"I am going to Munich," he said unexpectedly. "Then I go to Vienna for a conference."

We nodded politely and the conversation stopped. Men and women passengers were walking up and down the corridor and were soon invited into the reserved compartment. They bowed respectfully to the high S.S. officer, took their seats and gave our shabby clothes a scornful stare.

There was no further conversation about Holland. I was glad of this. My sole visit to that country had been the journey in the barge up the River Waal to Germany as a prisoner in 1940. As soon as the passengers began to snore, Luteyn stayed awake according to our arrangement and I slept for a few hours until his turn came to sleep. I was awakened by a loud tapping on the glass of the door and two military policemen looked in. They checked the passes of the soldiers and even scrutinised the documents of the S.S. officer. They stopped for a moment to stare at our queerly tailored clothes. I wondered for a moment whether they would recognise the colour of R.A.F. trousers, but the S.S. officer intervened importantly.

"These are foreign workers (*fremdarbeiter*). Dutch," he said with conviction.

The military police hesitated, then turned away as if suspicious civilians were nothing to do with their department. Now it was Luteyn's turn to sleep and I listened to the endless rattle of the express as we passed through Plauen and Hof and sped southwards into Bavaria. Lifting the blind, I glimpsed the snow outside or studied the sleeping faces in the dim light of the compartment. Towards four in the morning the train began to slow and came to a halt amid the sounds of a large station. I woke Luteyn, rose and stretched my limbs, and walked over to the doorway. In the gloom there was shouting and the bustle of passengers. I leant out of the window and saw on a sign before me the word "Regensburg."

It was here that we were due to change for the train to Ulm and we stepped on to the platform in the sharp cold.

"Good-bye, Dutchmen," said the S.S. man pompously from inside the compartment.

We went into a waiting-room and sat down at a table. Passengers with their luggage came with us, and promptly fell asleep with their heads resting on the tables. Opposite, a man in railway police uniform stared at us in unfriendly fashion. We did not wait for him to speak but walked out again on to the platform and entered the booking-hall. We sat on the floor with other travellers leaning against a wooden partition. A man and a girl smelling of spiced sausages and garlic lay near us in a close embrace.

When the train to Ulm had filled with passengers it left the station in a cloud of steam and we found seats in a compartment, again taking turns to keep awake. When dawn came I saw that we were travelling through the wintry countryside of Bavaria. The snow, collecting along the edges of the windows, framed a picture of white roofs and towers set in the hollows of the hills. Sometimes beside the track an *autobahn* stretched like a tape threading through the forests and long convoys of military vehicles moved into the mist.

At nine on the second morning of the escape the train drew into Ulm and we left it, making our way towards the booking office. Luteyn calmly asked the girl for two tickets to Singen on the Swiss frontier. She frowned and my heart began to sink. She asked for papers and we showed our papers to her.

"I must fetch the railway police. Stay here."

We did not wish to run away, hoping that our papers would satisfy them. A fat, red-faced railway policeman in his dark blue uniform asked us why we wished to go to the frontier zone. Luteyn explained that we were due to begin work in Ulm on the morrow and wished to spend a short vacation. The policeman, looking baffled, released us and we started to leave the station, walking across the big square in front. There was a shout behind us.

"Come back, gentlemen! I want to speak to you again."

The policeman took us to an office in the goods-yard where a thin, tight-lipped German railway police lieutenant sat at a desk. He examined our false papers with bewilderment. It appeared to me that the writing on it did not make sense to him. I could hardly stop myself from laughing as he lifted them to the light, looking, no doubt, for water marks. He was, however, impressed by Luteyn's Dutch passport and there seemed no inkling in his mind that we were escaped prisoners of war.

"I don't understand these men at all," he said helplessly. "Take them to the Labour Office. I wish someone would control these foreign workers more efficiently."

We walked across the square outside the station escorted by another policeman with a revolver. We chatted gaily in German, complimenting the man on the beauties of the town of Ulm. He was flattered and asked us about our own country of Holland. So much did we win his confidence that when we reached the State Labour Office, where men in brown uniforms with spades stood guard at the entrance, he bade us walk up the steps on our own, saying he would wait for us. His parting words were:

"You speak good German. Go and report to the office on the first floor and I shall wait for you here."

Smiling to ourselves and hardly able to believe our good fortune, we climbed to the top floor of the building and it was not long before we discovered some stairs on the far side from the entrance. Hurrying down them we left by another door. Avoiding the policeman and the guards with spades, we made for the back streets of Ulm, and Luteyn bought a map of the surrounding country in a small shop.

The cold had now become intense and, walking beyond the suburbs of Ulm, we left the snow-capped roofs of the university town behind us and hurried towards the town of Laupheim. It was nearly dusk when we reached the market-square and, asking the way to the station, we took tickets to Stockach, a village as near to the Swiss frontier as we dared to go. The country folk on the platform watched us in silence as we sat upon a bench sleepily waiting for the train. When it arrived we entered a wooden compartment too tired to be able to take turns to stay awake. The train jolted on into the night. We wakened only at the sound of a halt, and after passing the village of Pfullendorf we reached Stockach about nine in the evening.

Of Stockach I only remember white cottages in the moonlight and a doubtful station master watching us as we walked into the hills hoping to reach the frontier town of Singen when the moon went down and the frontier was in darkness. The road began to rise steeply through the forests and great banks of snow were on either side of us. Even by two o'clock in the morning we still had many miles to go, struggling along the icy road as the moon began to wane. The road slowly descended towards Singen.

It seemed hopeless to try to cross the frontier that night and we determined to look for somewhere to hide until the following evening. At five o'clock on the morning of January 8th, we were still moving towards Singen. Lights showed ahead of us in the roadway and to our tired eyes they seemed welcoming and kind. Then the figures of four men appeared. They were woodcutters walking to work from Singen. They hailed us and we wished them good morning. Something about us surprised them.

"Are you Poles?" said one of them.

"Yes," replied Luteyn.

"I don't believe it," said another. "Poles are not allowed out of their camp at five in the morning."

Evidently there was a Polish labour camp in the neighbourhood. The four woodcutters looked startled and undecided. As for me, I was near to surrender. My feet seemed to be frozen in my boots as if in blocks of ice. I hardly cared that we had come so far only to be recaptured. I could only think of warm fires and beds.

"Go, Hans, fetch the police," said the oldest woodcutter. The man called Hans who wheeled a bicycle, mounted it and rode off towards Singen. The remainder confronted us uncertainly. They did not try to detain us but stood irresolute and dumb. We suddenly realised that they were frightened of us. Without a word we dashed to the side of the road and into the forest, running in the snow until we sank exhausted. My breath came painfully and my head began to swim. I could not look at the whiteness around me without pain. We rose to our feet after a minute and began to move across a clearing. There was no sign of the woodcutters. As I walked there came over me a kind of delirium between sleep and waking. I thought that I was on some parade ground in England. I felt a figure beside me and turned to see my old Colonel marching in the snow in his uniform and field boots. I spoke to him and addressed him respectfully.

"What the hell?" said Luteyn.

"It's all right," I said ashamed.

Luteyn grunted impatiently, and a few paces across the clearing we came to a large wooden hut surrounded by a fence. There was the outline of a pathway, shrubs and flower beds in the snow, and beside the hut were beehives. We walked up to the hut and tried the doors which were all locked, but a small window in the wall was open. We lifted ourselves in and staggered crazily around the hut in the faint light of dawn. There was no sound of life. We found a kitchen and two rooms in one of which there was a bed. Tired and faint, we lay together on the bed in the intense cold and with an old blanket over us fell into a deep sleep, not waking until the afternoon.

When we awoke there had been another heavy fall of snow which luckily concealed our footsteps leading to the hut. From outside it seemed that we could hear the far-off sound of dogs and we got ready to escape into the woods. But as the hours passed no one came in sight and the sound of barking grew faint. Searching the hut, we found in one corner of the kitchen, spades and shovels, and hanging behind the door, two long white coats evidently used by the bee keeper.

According to our map, we were in the middle of a forest, two or three miles from Singen. We planned, therefore, to leave the hut at dusk and walk along the road to the town. West of the town and to the south lay woods through which ran the road and railway line to Schaffhausen in Switzerland. At some points the road formed the frontier between Switzerland and Germany.

Shortly before five o'clock on this afternoon of the eighth of January, we shouldered spades, and carrying the two white coats under our arms we cut through the forest to the road to Singen. For more than a mile we saw no one on the road, then the lights of bicycles came towards us and a voice called "Halt." In the glow of the bicycle lamps I could see two boys in the uniform of the Hitler Youth, each armed with truncheons. I felt no fear of them. Refreshed by sleep, I was determined they should not stop us. The boys spoke in a hectoring fashion.

"What are your names and where are you going?"

"We are Westphalians working in the neighbourhood and we are going back to our lodgings in Singen," said the resourceful Luteyn. This was a good choice of disguise for the Dutch accent resembles that of the Westphalians. The boys seemed doubtful.

"What is wrong?" I said, trying to imitate Luteyn's accent.

"We have been told to look for two British prisoners who have escaped and are thought to be trying to cross the frontier tonight."

We both laughed.

"They won't get far," said Luteyn, "it is much too cold for prisoners of war!"

The boys laughed uncertainly and rode off towards Singen and as we reached the town they turned again and came towards us. One said to the other:

"There are the Westphalians."

As this conversation was taking place in the road I reflected that these boys alone stood between us and freedom. Afterwards I asked Luteyn what was in his mind.

"For me to kill one with my spade and you the other," he said, "what did you intend to do?"

"Exactly the same."

We passed through Singen in the black-out, without incident, and skirting a great dark mound which seemed to be a slag heap we set off southwards through the wood, marching upon a compass bearing to the frontier. At two o'clock in the morning on the ninth of January we crossed the railway to Schaffhausen about two miles north of a point where the road forms the frontier. It was a fine, cold night and the moon was full. Wrapping ourselves in the white bee-keepers coats for camouflage, we slowly advanced until we could see a gap in the trees and lights of cars passing along the road ahead. Not far to the east were voices and lanterns and what appeared to be a frontier post.

For an hour we crouched in a ditch beside the road and

watched a sentry pacing up and down only forty yards away. Here we ate the remainder of our chocolate and swallowed a few mouthfuls of snow. Black clouds began to hide the moon and the cold increased with a rising wind. I watched the German buttoning the collar of his overcoat and saw him move towards the sentry-box beside the frontier barrier.

Before us across the roadway was a smooth plain of snow surrounded by distant trees. Beyond this few hundred yards of open No Man's Land was freedom. At half-past four in the morning the sentry turned away from us. I could no longer hear his footsteps against the wind.

"Do you agree to cross now?" said Luteyn.

"This is the moment," I whispered.

We crawled from the ditch and across the road still dressed in our white coats. We continued crawling across the field in front of us, ploughing on hands and knees through the deep snow. After what seemed an eternity we rose to our feet, and surged forward into Switzerland.

CHAPTER IX

OVER the Swiss frontier, we came to very deep snowdrifts through which we stumbled and sometimes sank, having to drag each other to our feet. Ahead were neither huts nor frontier guards, nothing to point the way to safety. At this point the territory of Switzerland is a narrow appendix forming a no-man's land before the first Swiss village is reached. Three hundred yards to the east a single lamp flickered ominously. We dared not approach it. We could not be sure that it did not shine in a German frontier post. We had to march due south on an accurate compass bearing to avoid blundering back into the enemy. Striving to maintain our reason after the nightmare of our escape, we stopped every few steps to check our bearings.

So tired were my limbs that I could hardly lift my feet. My boots were weighed down with ice. Often we were both waist-deep in snow. Sometimes neither of us could go further and for minutes lay panting and cursing.

Luteyn, so calm and resourceful through these perilous

days, began to talk despairingly in Dutch and seemed to be wandering in his mind. I pulled him from a deep drift where only his ski cap showed against that cruel whiteness. Then it was my turn to flounder, helpless and distraught, murmuring with a last attempt at humour that Patriotism was not enough.

It was an hour before we had travelled a quarter of a mile and found ourselves on higher ground. There came to us the sound of cow bells, and a clock chimed the hour of five in sweet tones. Under our feet we felt with unspeakable relief the welcome surface of a road. Suddenly, there were shadowy walls on either side. There was a row of small farmhouses and cow sheds. A single question tortured us. Were we in Switzerland? The buildings, faintly discerned, began to form a street with a church tower at its farthest end. The snow crunched loudly beneath our feet as we went by bounds from doorway to doorway watching and listening in terrible anxiety. I saw a blurred whiteness against the wall of a barn and I lit my petrol lighter. Pushing aside the snow, I could see an advertisement for a circus. There were elephants and tigers in gay colours and a ring-master with long moustaches. And then, with pounding heart, I sought the place of the performance. It was Schaffhausen, and we were at the Swiss village of Ramsen. We had come through!

We were the children who travelled beyond the Blue Mountains. We had reached the Promised Land. I thought of kneeling in the snow and thanking God for our deliverance. But there was little time for emotion. As we shook hands, the church clock of Ramsen struck a quarter-past five and there came the crisp sound of heavy boots along the street.

We dashed into the shadows, watching in a torment of fear for the familiar steel helmet of a German guard. A tall man walked nonchalantly towards us. He wore a long, heavy green overcoat, a pointed hat with black band turned up at one side, and he carried a rifle. I recognized immediately that he was a Swiss frontier guard serenely patrolling the village. My heart was beating so that I could hardly breathe. He came within a few yards and then we showed ourselves, appearing quietly before him. Startled, the guard took the rifle from his shoulder and pointed it at us.

"Halt! Who goes there?"

"Friends."

"Are you English?"

"Yes, and Dutch."

Then I could see that the guard was smiling. With shouts of joy we flung ourselves upon him shaking him by the hand and patting his back. Then Luteyn, the guard with his rifle on his shoulder, and I clasped each other's hands and danced in the snow, pirouetting and leaping first one way, then the other, so that the whole street echoed with our cheering. Lights came at the windows and voices asking in Swiss-German what it was all about. The little street seemed to be alive with our happiness. The guard shouted merrily, as if he was the most delighted man in the world, that we had escaped the tyranny of Hitler. Despite the cold and the early hour the people clapped hands as they leaned from their windows.

The three of us came to the Swiss frontier post and waited for an official to be roused from his bed. Standing beside a wood fire in the office, the sense of freedom surged through my veins like a cordial. Never in my life, perhaps, will I ever know such a moment of triumph. Without weapons we had pitted our wits against the might of Nazism and cheated the Germans in all their self-conscious arrogance and cruelty. How bitterly I hated them! I looked at Luteyn. He was asleep in a chair beside the fire clasping a frost-bitten finger in his handkerchief. I smiled. He looked like a child worn out after a long day at the seaside or the Zoo.

Soon came a kindly Swiss official who seated himself at a high desk. Taking a pen he wrote our names and particulars in a book and asked us whether there was anyone in Switzerland who could vouch for us. I was able to give the name of Madame Paravicini, the wife of the former Swiss Minister in London. She had sent me letters and parcels for several months bringing hope and comfort to me as she had to hundreds of others.

When these simple formalities were over we walked with the guard to the police station of Ramsen where clean comfortable beds were prepared and great steaming cups of chocolate laced with brandy were handed to us. Then in a warm feeling of contentment, hardly able to comprehend our whereabouts, we lay down on the beds and slept until dawn.

I was awakened by the entry of a rosy Swiss policeman. He asked if I should like to shave and wash. He lent me a razor and I moved over to a mirror and looked into it. Was this the great escaper, or some dejected inmate of a casual ward turned out upon the road? My face was grey and unshaven and my lips were black and cracked, but my feet though chapped and sore were not blistered. On my ears were large red chilblains. My eyes were still defiant but there was fear in them. I still felt faint, but gradually recovering, began to shave with earnest concentration. I put on my blue jacket and miserable ski cap, now dried by the police station fire. I looked at myself once more in the mirror and now there was a twinkle in my eyes. Then came a police sergeant with brandy and coffee and rolls and good fresh butter. Luteyn was still asleep. Then he, too, was wakened and shaved himself. At nine in the morning of the ninth of January, 1942, we were taken by a plain-clothes officer to the train for Schaffhausen. Just eighty-four hours had passed since we escaped from Colditz.

We sat in the train beside the plain-clothes man and watched the morning sun rise over the Swiss fields. After a short journey, the officer grinned and pointed to the name of a station. My blood ran cold. We were at a German frontier station. The plain-clothes man laughed and told us not to be afraid for it was a Swiss train travelling for a short way through German territory to Schaffhausen.

As the train sped back through Switzerland, Luteyn and I talked happily in English like children going home for the school holiday. Beside us an elderly woman in black clothes listened to our talk and gave us a gracious bow. I recalled then that train journey to Colditz in 1941 and the indignant gaze of the Herr Hauptmann and his wife Hilde. A Swiss officer standing in the corridor heard us too, and, as he left the train at Schaffhausen, he smiled, clicked his heels and gave a smart salute.

Police headquarters in Schaffhausen was a pleasant clean place with a roaring fire. We sat first in a waiting room and then one by one were taken for interrogation into the main office. The police officers spoke little English and the whole of my interrogation was conducted in French. They asked me little of a military nature and seemed only interested in conditions in Germany. There was not much I could tell them for a prisoner of war seeking to avoid contact with the people in enemy territory can judge little of their standard of life, but I spoke feelingly upon the shortage of chocolate. At the end of my interrogation I delivered a long peroration upon the Germans in general to the great amusement of the police. I referred to them as *Boches*.

"Please do not refer to the Germans as *Boches*, Lieutenant Neave. You must remember that we are neutral," said a police official and winked discreetly. "You will be under Hotel arrest for a few days," he said.

"Hotel arrest," involved confinement in a small but comfortable hotel in the centre of Schaffhausen. We arrived there about twelve o'clock and straightway sat down in a restaurant with blue check table cloths, and ordered a steak apiece and a bottle of wine. The proprietor joined us in celebration and very shortly I was so drunk that I spoke no connected language, mixing in my sentences German, French, English and even a smattering of Polish. The good proprietor, seeing the effect of alcohol upon escaped prisoners, ushered us upstairs to a room with two pure white beds where we lay down and immediately lost consciousness.

Those halcyon days of "hotel arrest" passed swiftly. The snow fell in big flakes outside as I sat in the warm restaurant and watched the people passing in the street. Each morning we drank coffee with the customers and talked of the war. The hostility of the German Swiss to the Nazis was intense and they were anxious to listen to our tales of horror and persecution. We waxed eloquent over the wine and cognac in German and French. As the day wore on more customers came to buy us drinks and share our fuddled happiness. The prison camp had long disappeared from my consciousness. It served only as a medium for conversation and for picturesque accounts of my adventures with which I regaled solid Swiss commercial travellers.

I fear that "security" meant little to me at this time and that the possibility that any of these cheerful-looking gentlemen could be an agent of the Nazis had not occurred to me. I was happy in their company. But often, when the haze of cigar smoke cleared away, there were memories of my fellow prisoners, left behind in the castle of Colditz. Buying two picture post cards of Schaffhausen from the proprietor, I borrowed an ancient pen and began to write. The first I addressed to a prisoner in the camp and signed it with an assumed name. I wrote a short message, previously agreed, to indicate our safe arrival in Switzerland. The other post-card showed Swiss girls in a traditional dance. This I addressed in English to the Kommandant of Oflag IVc, Oberst Prawitz, Colditz, near Leipzig, Germany. I began:

"Dear Oberst, I am glad to be able to inform you that my friend and I have arrived safely for our holiday in Switzerland. We had a pleasant journey, suffering the minimum of inconvenience. I hope that you will not get sent to the Russian Front on my account. My regards to Hauptmann Priem. Yours sincerely, A. M. S. Neave, Lieutenant, Royal Artillery."

We did not send either postcard for some weeks after our escape, for there was so far no sign of John Hyde-Thomson and Lieutenant Donkers. Years afterwards I heard what had happened. When the officials at Ulm learned of our disappearance from the State Labour Office they established a stronger control at the railway station. The arrival of two more "Dutch electrical workers" asking for tickets to the frontier zone was too much for the bewildered railway police. John Hyde-Thomson and his friend were arrested, forced to disclose their identity and taken back to Colditz. I should like to be certain that the Oberst received his postcard. It must have riled his Prussian soul.

Just when we were beginning to grow impatient with our detention in the hotel, a policeman came and told us to pack. We were driven in a police car to the station of Schaff-hausen. This time the train travelled south avoiding German territory and arrived at Berne where we were delivered to our respective Legations.

I was taken through a garden door to a small house beside the Legation used by the British Military and Air Attachés. I waited humbly in a small cold room until Colonel Cart-wright, the hero of many escapes in the first world war and Military Attaché at Berne, advanced to shake me by the hand. I was taken into the cellar of the Legation and shown a stack of clothing suitable for refugees and from this I chose an awful green tweed suit of Swiss design. Nothing could have given me a greater inferiority complex in the well-tailored atmosphere of the Legation. However, since I could not continue to move in diplomatic circles dressed as a "Dutch electrician," I was grateful for the tweed monstrosity.

My first night in Berne was spent at Colonel Cartwright's flat where I was treated with sympathy and kindness and then for a night or two I lived with the Assistant Military Attaché, Major Fryer and his wife.

Being among English people living civilised lives disturbed me. I wanted to be alone with my confused emotions. In the mornings I walked to the Legation for various papers to be put in order, endlessly smoking small cheroots called *Stumpen* for which I conceived an eccentric passion. I smoked them from morn till night, and as I smoked I looked around me, wide-eyed at the sights and sounds of Berne. Several days passed before I became accustomed to the traffic. Often, like some old and helpless man, I was afraid to cross the street.

A summons came to attend the doctor for a medical examination. Beneath cloistered arches I found the house of Doctor von Erlach who was a physician and a high official of the Swiss Red Cross. As an attendant opened the door of the surgery I was dazzled by a sudden flash of instruments and white bowls. A tall man in gold-rimmed spectacles walked forward and held out his hand.

"So we meet again, Mr. Neave."

For a moment, I looked at him without understanding, then I dimly remembered a day at Spangenburg back in 1941 when a Swiss delegation visited the camp and I was summoned to receive a message from home. Doctor von Erlach in the sky-blue uniform of a Colonel in the Swiss Army was standing in the grim hospital of the camp surrounded by German officers. I, in an old battledress and sweater, came to meet the Doctor and his deputation. I wore an inadequate beard which made me resemble an old photograph of my grandfather when he was an undergraduate. Von Erlach smiled at me from his great height and, speaking kindly, said:

"I have a special message from Madame Paravicini that your family are well and send you their love." I walked back into the camp and paced beside the barbed wire looking towards the distant hills.

*   *   *   *

On this day in January of the following year, the Doctor examined me briskly but found no serious injury. He prescribed three weeks' rest in the country, and I was sent to his home not far away from Berne, a charming chalet known as Rosengarten, near Gertzensee. Sitting before the fire for many days while the snow fell unceasingly, I would pat the head of a great sheep dog and puff away at my *Stumpen*. I did not read books for my thoughts were too full of stimulating events. What was to happen next? When I had recovered from the physical effects of the escape from Colditz I felt a great restlessness. My success in reaching Switzerland was the summit of all my hopes. I had not turned my thoughts to the future in store for me beyond that last desperate surge over the frontier. Nothing could ever equal that matchless moment in the streets of Ramsen. I waited, hoping that the end of my adventure would not bring disillusionment.

It was at Rosengarten that I spent my twenty-fifth birthday. The weeks that followed were passed in the university town of Fribourg where I stayed at an hotel under the surveillance of the Swiss police. I lived a life of mild dissipation, made many friends among the Polish officers interned in the neighbourhood, became entangled with a number of alleged female spies and attended one lecture on architecture at Fribourg University.

In early April, 1942, when the daffodils grew wild among the woods near Fribourg and the fields were covered with bright green grass, I received an urgent summons to Geneva. I was told to leave my luggage in the care of an unsuspecting Swiss, and slunk off to the station.

I sat in the train to Geneva wondering what new phase in this personal drama was at hand. I knew that plans were being made for escaped British prisoners to leave Switzerland in secrecy, but I knew no details. My orders were to meet a man wearing a dark felt hat, who would be reading a Swiss periodical outside the station at Geneva.

As I came down the steps of the station, I saw the man leaning against a newspaper kiosk. He seemed to be so conspicuous that I felt he might just as well have carried a small banner with the words "Secret Agent." As I came close, he looked up expectantly, and I could see that he was reading the periodical upside down!

"*Je viens de la part d'Aristide!*" said I.

"Come and have a drink, mon lieutenant," said the man without giving any answer to the password. We wandered to an inconspicuous bar in a side street. We both drank Pernod and, in a slight daze, I learned that I was to escape over the Swiss frontier early next morning with Captain Hugh Woollatt, M.C. of the Lancashire Fusiliers. For the next twenty-four hours I lived in an atmosphere of high melodrama.

Hugh Woollatt was a regular officer. He was tall with a thin face and rather long dark hair, which gave him a care-free appearance, particularly when he wore a beret basque. He was very alert and a courageous man having escaped from an Oflag at Bibrach not far from the Swiss border in 1941. His sense of humour was an asset to both of us in the arduous journey which followed our meeting. It is sad to record that he was killed in action in Normandy in July, 1944. He was not the only escaper to lose his life shortly after reaching England. Among the eleven successful British and Empire escapers from Colditz, Squadron Leader H. N. Fowler, M.C., R.A.F., who broke out of a German Sergeant-Major's office window and reached Switzerland in 1942, was killed flying two years later. Major R. B. Littledale, D.S.O., of the K.R.R.C., who escaped at the same time as Pat Reid in October, 1942, was killed in action in Normandy in August, 1944.

I parted from the "agent" who referred to himself as Robert, arranging to meet him later in the day, and, on his instructions, met Hugh Woollatt at a tumbledown hotel where we were to stay the night. I took with me a little suitcase full of clothes which Robert had given me. Hugh Woollatt gaily informed me that, in his opinion, "only the odd man on a bicycle" was unaware of our secret hiding place. As we talked an old crone crept down the creaking stairs of the hotel and pushed a registration book in front of us.

"What on earth do we do now?" I asked.

"Write a false name, old boy, as if you were staying here with a tart," said Woollatt.

I laughed and promptly wrote my name as Oscar Wilde.

As I handed the book to the ancient proprietress I thought I detected a faint smile as she peered at our signatures, for Woollatt had described himself as Herr Albert Hall.

Walking by the Lake of Geneva in the sunshine of a spring evening, we again met Robert of the dark hat. He discoursed, with several vague allusions to our journey, on the dangers of travelling through Vichy France. I did not enquire how our escape had been arranged. The man made clear to both of us that we were not expected to ask questions but to obey orders.

Wishing us good luck he vanished and we sought a restaurant.

After a large meal of very hot curry and rice washed down with lager, we found our way back to the rickety hotel and clambered up a flight of wooden stairs to a bedroom on the top floor. At midnight we checked the papers and money which Robert had given to both of us. My peregrinations over Europe had resulted in yet another change of identity. This time I had a French identity card for a Czech refugee in the Unoccupied Zone of France. My photograph was one taken of me shortly after my arrival in Berne and far from flattering. These papers purported to allow me to travel to Marseilles but why a citizen of Czechoslovakia had any business in that town was not stated. The clothes which had been given us were a great improvement on those I had worn on previous escapes. I now had a shabby genteel blue suit and a cloth cap which gave me a sense of dignity.

Zero hour for our departure from the hotel was, according to Robert, half-past three in the morning. We were told only to expect a Swiss policeman to fetch us. Months of experience as prisoners had made us distrustful even of our helpers. We waited to challenge anyone who came up the hotel stairs. We lay down on the beds but could not sleep listening for the sound of the car. I heard the squeal of brakes and moved over to the window. A clock in the town struck half-past three. A large black car had drawn up outside the hotel and I saw two men leave it. They were big men in dark hats and coats, and as I watched, I heard them knock at the door of the hotel. Then came voices.

Footsteps echoed up the stairs and there was a plaintive croaking from the proprietress below. Softly I opened the window. Ten feet below was a flat roof, an easy way of escape. A faint tap on the door and a tall man in a mackintosh, like some Continental hero of detective fiction, strode into the room and gave the password. We laughed with relief, picked up diminutive suitcases, part of the equipment we had received from Robert and, entering the car with two plain-clothes and two uniformed Swiss police, drove swiftly out of Geneva.

As the police car sped southwards, the dawn revealed mountain peaks and the shores of the Lake Geneva. I felt liverish and inadequate after an excess of curry on the previous evening. The car stopped near a small cemetery and there, with the police officer, we crouched among the graves underneath a wall of flints. As I lay in the grass, spots swam before my eyes like a swarm of bees. They looked as if they were encircling a horrible ornate monument to the dead which stood a yard away. Over the cemetery wall was a great broad carpet of wire dividing France from Switzerland.

"All is arranged on the other side," said the tall man in a mackintosh who had given us the password at the hotel. "You have only to go across the wire and stand by the signpost to Annemasse. Remember us to Mr. Churchill."

At five o'clock exactly, leaving the police officer crouching in the dew of the cemetery, Woollatt and I vaulted the wall, crawled a few paces through the grass and then climbed slowly over the broad mesh of barbed wire. As I crossed the last strand there was an awful rending sound and I felt the cool morning air upon my thighs. I turned to see a substantial piece of my trousers clinging to the frontier defences. A muffled laugh came from behind the cemetery wall. We were now in France, and as we crouched beside a hedge, Woollatt lent me his raincoat to conceal the gap in my trousers.

When we reached the signpost to Annemasse the road was full of cyclists. We had been told to meet at 5.30 a.m. a man wearing a blue smock and sabots, riding a bicycle and smoking a clay pipe upside down who would act as our guide. To our dismay this was a very fair description of practically every man to be seen upon the roads of the Haute Savoie in the early morning. As we stood by the signpost at least twenty men wearing smocks and sabots and smoking clay pipes cycled past upon their way to work. We were beginning to despair of making contact with our guide when a middle-aged man of distinguished appearance leapt off his bicycle and, removing an inverted clay pipe from his mouth, bowed low and respectfully. We exchanged passwords.

"Good morning, gentlemen" said the man in perfect English with an air of great dignity, as if he were about to take our orders for an expensive breakfast, "I am sorry to be late. Let me introduce myself—I am Louis, formerly of the Ritz Hotel, London."

CHAPTER X

Louis had a square forehead and silver-grey hair. I could picture him in a black tail coat attending to hotel guests with dignified assurance. His blue smock did not disguise the essential grace of his movements. He spoke easily giving us directions with quiet efficiency. It was my first experience of the French Résistance and I was greatly moved by his obvious courage.

And yet my escape now seemed to have reached an anti-climax. There were, it is true, many dangers to be overcome in the journey before me and I knew I should encounter much bravery and devotion which would be inspiring, but it did not seem that any further personal achievement could match that sense of triumph I had on crossing from Germany into Switzerland. I was never again to organise my own escape; to concentrate for hours on my plans, separating the practical from the impractical; to collect material for uniforms or other disguises. The future plans had been made by others. All I had to do was to obey the orders of the guides. I knew that Hugh Woollatt felt the same but we were determined, out of admiration for the gallant people who helped us, to obey them implicitly.

Louis looked at our clothes with a quizzical expression on his fine features.

"Your disguise is not good. You look the perfect gentlemen."

"We are supposed to be Czechs," I said.

Louis grimaced. He began to tell us of his life as a waiter at the Ritz in the years before the war and about the small property in the shadow of the mountains which he now owned. We walked by his side towards the frontier town of Annemasse. His dark eyes shone with excitement as he wheeled his bicycle through the no-man's land between Switzerland and the unoccupied zone of Vichy France.

"I shall take you past the frontier post in a few minutes. We shall come upon it suddenly at a bend in the road."

We walked through lines of poplars, and soon the wind blew and the rain swept across the paved roadway. Far ahead I could see a sentry box and a French *douanier* in a cape watching men and women as they struggled through the rain. Woollatt and I, aided by the storm, mingled with the crowd, and passed the control post with bowed heads. Louis ignored us, and wheeling his bicycle up to the *douanier* engaged the man in laughing conversation. I could hear him shouting behind us against the sound of rain and muddy water swirling in the gutters.

A mile beyond the frontier, the storm passed swiftly, leaving the mountain tops shrouded in grey mist. Louis, rejoining us, led the way to a new brick house. A powerful smell of frying food overpowered the scent of spring flowers drenched with rain. In the kitchen a great breakfast awaited us. The table was spread with a paper cloth adorned with blue polka dots on it and there was ham and toast and splendid coffee. A huge dish of eggs fried in butter was swiftly set before us by a kindly woman, Louis' wife. She, too, had fine grey hair, and the manners of a duchess.

"I have prepared a special London breakfast for you," she said proudly. Her handsome face was pale and I saw there were lines beneath her eyes. Her voice faltered a little as she said:

"I have not slept the whole night in case something should go wrong. Thank God you have got this far."

The muslined windows of the kitchen were tightly shut and I was near to collapse from the heat and the smell of cooking. My appetite had been impaired by my last meal of curry in Geneva and the excitement which had turned my stomach. I dared not refuse her hospitality and swallowed the eggs and coffee. Spots circled before my eyes thicker than ever, and I searched for a means of escape into the cool sweet air. A knock at the door came as a welcome and hopeful diversion. A young girl entered, her head covered in a blanket.

She removed the blanket revealing long black hair. Her face was very white as if she had spent her life in the shadows of a cloister. The forehead was high and the black hair parted in the centre. Her nose was sharp, a little ugly, and her mouth too hard for beauty. She sat quietly at the table for a moment and then spoke to Louis. Her voice had the tone of a vesper bell.

"All is ready," she said, gravely. Louis turned to us.

"Mademoiselle Jeanne is your next guide. She will take you to the other side of the town. I myself am responsible only for the first lap. We expect two more 'parcels' to-morrow. But please, gentlemen, finish your breakfast. You have half an hour at least before you must leave."

The struggle against the desire to vomit passed as I watched the girl. Her eyes were cast down as if in prayer. She said nothing until she rose, ready to go. Then I saw her face clearly. Her eyes had the fervour of a deep faith, and in her sallow features were the lines of suffering willingly borne. She restored the blanket to her head and turned to the door with solemn grace.

We walked with Mademoiselle Jeanne through allotments and smallholdings into Annemasse. We two, light-hearted and often cynical, were afraid to speak, so deeply had her faith impressed us. In a side-street, she knocked on the door of a decrepit house where another young, sad-faced French woman led us through a dark passage to a kitchen. The smell of frying met us once more and caught me cruelly by the throat. Fried eggs were ready in profusion and the young woman seemed prepared to out-do Louis' wife in the size of her English breakfast. Sick and perspiring, I drank two further cups of coffee and with enormous effort swallowed more fried eggs. An hour passed without conversation. A small child played beside us in the stuffy kitchen. Sitting at the table, Mademoiselle Jeanne seemed as if carved in stone, the figure of a saint in meditation. Once I ventured to ask a question about our escape route and its organisers. She lifted her eyes reproachfully.

"All I ask of you is that you should send a message on the

B.B.C. if you get back to England in safety," she said. "Here everyone listens to the B.B.C."

Her olive cheeks glowed faintly and she spoke with a sudden warmth. Her eyes for a moment held mine. In their strange sacrificial light I read no womanly interest in myself or Woollatt. There was mystic devotion and courage which placed her far above the desires of the world. Virginal and fanatical, Mademoiselle Jeanne fought her lone intense battle against the powers of darkness without fear. Her work for the French Résistance was but a part of an inner struggle of the spirit. Like other heroines of the great Resistance Movement she inspired the respect and reverence of those she helped. With her there could be neither intimacy nor companionship.

We sat listening to the loud ticking of the kitchen clock. Suddenly there came a knocking on the door. Through the passage into the kitchen, came a round-faced man, addressed by Mademoiselle Jeanne as Alex. He informed us that he had come with his car to take us to Annecy on the next stage of our journey. He asked for our papers.

"Czechs? But this is ridiculous! Why are you supposed to be Czechs?"

We had no idea and felt embarrassed and unhappy. Alex shrugged his shoulders and muttered some criticism of the "Chief" whose identity we were never able to discover. He waited impatiently while we said good-bye to the sad housewife and her child. At the doorway, Mademoiselle Jeanne had veiled herself again in the blanket against the newly falling rain. She did not smile, but shook my hand quite fiercely as she said good-bye, and turning away walked slowly along the street.

In the splendid scenery of Upper Savoy, an ancient Citroën driven by Alex rattled us along the road to Annecy. Alex was a cheerful, plump person much occupied with the Black Market. He had sleek black hair and his dress was a little flashy. No more profound contrast with the saintly Jeanne could be imagined. He chattered away as he drove, speaking of the methods he employed to outwit the authorities. Yet he was a patriot and an efficient organiser.

Passing Ugines, we soon came to the shore of the great lake of Annecy and glimpsed its glorious blue water bathed in sunshine. The snow glistened on the mountains as the road wound among picturesque villages at their foot. Sometimes the engine of the car driven by a charcoal burner or *gasogène* began to choke and gasp, and once, after a sharp explosion, the car came to a stop. Then we heard a treble horn in the distance, and a vehicle, flashing a light careered towards us.

"The flicks!" exclaimed Alex. "Save yourselves! I will stay with the car. They will not worry about me. I am well known in the Black Market."

We ran panting through bushes beside the shore of the Lake and waited, listening. There were voices, but the police car, still sounding its shrill horn, moved off. The Citroen, which Alex had repaired, started off again with a jolt, travelling along the quayside of Annecy past medieval buildings and holiday hotels shuttered and forlorn. It entered a big square with a splendid view of the distant mountains, and, bouncing over the *pavé*, came to rest beneath an archway.

"This," said Alex, "is the house of Pierre and Cécile."

I smiled faintly. I feared another vast meal inside my overloaded stomach. I was not disappointed. Climbing gloomy wooden stairs, we came to a dismal three-roomed flat. Cécile was in the kitchen. She was about thirty and had a round face resembling a pink cake of soap.

Her lips and nails were thickly painted red and her hands were shaking as she prepared the meal.

Cécile was a different type of heroine from the saintly Mademoiselle Jeanne. She had none of her apparent indifference to danger. Cécile was nervous and twittering, with little strength of purpose, bracing herself to follow the lead of an adventurous young husband. She could not conceal her fear of the consequences of helping Allied officers to escape. As she prepared our meal she seemed to be listening, pausing for a moment as she moved across the room like a frightened animal. No stern idealism was there to reinforce her failing courage. A sense of family duty alone kept her from panic. She was courageous in her weakness, seeking to struggle on for the sake of her husband.

I was absorbed with interest in our helpers as they sat around the table.

These men and women were among the first to organise an escape route from the Swiss frontier to Spain. In the spring of 1942, the Vichy Government still retained control of Unoccupied France. Their police arrested sympathisers of de Gaulle and flung Allied soldiers into prison camps. Yet these early flames of Résistance burned brightly in a few brave hearts. With the coming of German occupation in November, 1942, the whole people banded together against the enemy in groups waiting for the hour to strike. Sabotage and the well-organised collection of intelligence was widespread in Savoy. Escape organisations grew in number all over France and succeeded in returning hundreds of captured Allied servicemen to the fight.

The meal lasted long into the afternoon and finished with cognac and other liqueurs.

"Now," said Alex to Hugh Woollatt and myself, "let us be serious. I will take you in the car to Chambéry with Pierre before it is dark. From there we accompany you in the train to Marseilles. Please do exactly as we ask you."

"Are our Czech papers any use?" said Woollatt.

"I remember hearing," said Alex, "that there are many Czech refugees in Marseilles. You must say if the police stop us that you are going to a reception centre."

I wondered in some confusion what sort of "reception centre" for foreign nationals existed under the Vichy Government.

"They are called *centres d'accueil*," said Alex. "Do not worry, we shall get you to safety."

I could see that he was nervous and irritated by our doubts. Perhaps there was some sense of ingratitude that we British should ask so many questions. I concealed my own anxiety, changing the subject to the iniquities of Marshal Petain.

As was talked, there came the sound of sobbing from the dingy kitchen. It grew louder until all conversation ceased. Pierre, the husband, was annoyed. He seemed to be a hot-headed person. High spirited and adventurous, he resented his wife's timidity. He led her back beside the table on which empty wine bottles still stood, and the air was heavy with the smell of Gauloise cigarettes.

"Be quiet, you will ruin everything!" he cried.

We were silent feeling that we were the cause of her suffering. Alex said good-bye to her as she choked back her sobs. We followed him down the worn stairs and saw her tear-stained face as she stood forlorn and defenceless at the doorway of the flat. With Alex at the wheel and Pierre sitting gloomily at his side, the Citroen rattled away from Annecy, and at dusk we came to Chambéry. At a house near the station a spare, anonymous woman entertained us while we waited for the train to Marseilles.

I was wearing the suit given to me at Geneva and a French cap of tweed. Woollatt had a grey Homburg hat slightly too small for him. Safe in the darkness, we attracted no attention from Admiral Darlan's special police two of whom patrolled the station. Trains were few and far between, and the crowd on the platform was immense. Surrounded by quantities of untidy luggage they stood and gesticulated as the Marseilles express drew to a standstill. Soon every carriage was crammed and eventually, well behind its scheduled time, the train jerked from the station to a chorus of complaints from those left behind upon the platform. With our luggage, consisting of two ancient brief-cases, the four of us easily forced our way into a carriage. It seemed absurd to me that I should be hiding from the French police in a country where two years before I had come to fight as an ally. And yet I feared the Frenchmen of Vichy almost as much as the Germans. In Germany, I could assume that no man was my friend. In the Unoccupied zone of France no one knew who could be trusted. During the night a young cadet of the military organisation set up by Darlan, known as the Milice, stood beside me in the corridor where I had forced my way in search of air. He was a loud, suspicious youth wearing an enormous, ungainly beret. He had those staring blue eyes I had seen in so many Nazis. I was next to him, unable to escape. Fear of this boy surged through me. Though I spoke good French, I did not trust my "Czech" cover story. I looked unhappily at Alex, who elbowed his way into the corridor and engaged the young collaborator in conversation.

Even for Alex, a true *débrouillard*, it was a risky task. No country is more dangerous to the underground worker than that in which loyalties are divided. I would always prefer to travel on a clandestine mission through enemy territory where every man's hand is against me. I forced my way back into the compartment and sat wedged between two sleeping passengers in the place where Alex had left. I closed my eyes and listened for their voices through the open door of the compartment. As the train sped on towards Marseilles I was heartened to hear the young man say to Alex,

"Vous êtes colaborateur, donc?"

At dawn, we reached Marseilles and hustling from the filthy train, handed over our tickets without incident. Walking on the boulevards, in the early morning sunshine I felt relieved at having escaped from the dangers of the train. I could now hide among the dark streets from the Police of Darlan.

We began to seek an address near the Canebière. Pierre and Alex were agitated and silent. Through dark passages filled with refuse, we sought the mysterious house where with the aid of the password we should find shelter before the next stage of our journey to Spain. We climbed an iron staircase in a disreputable block of flats and talked with a gargantuan prostitute.

When it was clear that we were not customers, she flew into a rage and leaning over a worn balcony shrieked foul language at us as we climbed down into the street, to pick our way through cabbage stalks, dead rats and rivulets of dirty water to the Canebière.

Robert at Geneva had given us an alternative address and password. Thus did we come to the café of Gaston. It was a small neat place with a row of painted tables down each side of a sawdust passage. Beyond was a pair of double doors with frosted glass. A waiter came towards us, motioning us to a table. As we sat there, I could see a young gendarme walking slowly past the entrance. He seemed to be looking into the café. The customers, working people wearing caps, spoke in low voices, eyeing us over their glasses of wine. This worried our French escorts. I turned to the waiter and softly asked him for Gaston. He looked at me in terror and disappeared. Then came a small, bald man who ushered us in silence from the table to a room, behind the double doors, at the end of the café. It was a square room with a large skylight and ancient furniture upholstered in green satin. It looked like an out-dated photographer's studio. We sat down obediently, and the bald man turned to us and peremptorily demanded the password. We both repeated it perfectly like a catechism. He seemed satisfied and tapped on a side door. To our consternation, a youthful gendarme entered and saluted sheepishly. It was the same gendarme that I had seen outside.

"Who is this?" I cried fearing a trap.

"Who is this?" said the bald man sourly. "Mind your own business. This is Jacques. He will fetch someone to talk to you. I regret the suspicious way in which all four of you barged into my café. I am not certain of your identity." Pierre and Alex flushed angrily.

We waited uncomfortably for the new character to make his appearance. The bald man, relenting a little, sent for coffee and drinks until we were all in a mellow mood. Slowly I realised that he had been deeply embarrassed by our clumsy arrival.

There was a knock on the frosted glass. A slim man of middle age dressed in a smart grey double-breasted suit and green pork-pie hat entered the room. His keen grey eyes surveyed us anxiously for a moment.

"The password please," he said in English.

His accent, though French, had a flavour of Throgmorton Street and of London clubs. We repeated the password obediently in our best French.

A friendly light began to dance in the man's eyes. He paced the room asking questions in English about Geneva, Louis, and Mademoiselle Jeanne while all the while our escorts, Pierre and Alex, sat glumly beside us not understanding a word.

"You can call me Maurice, you chaps," he said with his fingers to his lips in mock secrecy. He wore a dark red bow tie with white spots and his grey suit and suede shoes were clearly bought in London. Then he did a curious little *pas seul* around an old-fashioned armchair.

"When you get back I hope you will take some messages for me to my solicitors. I wanted to send a bottle of champagne to my brokers but I doubt if you will get that past the Pyrenees!" He slapped his thigh and laughed heartily.

I looked at Maurice in amazement as he twisted his neat grey moustache. I found it difficult to believe that he was real. No character in my adventures had seemed quite so confusing, accustomed as I had become to events too strange for fiction. Yet everything he said rang with sincerity. His good humour bubbled over, filling the gloomy back room. The bald man and even Pierre and Alex were soon won over by his gaiety. There was much laughter at the expense of Pierre Laval.

"There must be something wrong about a man who always wears a long white tie," said Maurice, crossing his knees and eyeing his suede shoes.

To Hugh Woollatt and myself this seemed to dismiss Pierre Laval for ever from a place in history. Yet sometimes through this light-hearted conversation there came a note of warning of the consequences if any of us fell into the hands of Vichy. I do not know if the true story of Maurice's work for the Allies will ever be written. He had business interests in the City of London before the war which enabled him to speak of it familiarly. Hugh Woollatt and I soon realised that Maurice was one of the most faithful and devoted workers of the *Résistance*. He was rich and could, if he had wished, have stayed away from the struggle. But he was a Frenchman who served the Allies with great courage and paid the penalty of long imprisonment by the Germans. At the end of the war he deservedly received a high decoration.

After discussing the City of London and the merits of Pimms No. 1 we said farewell to Pierre and Alex. We followed Maurice from the café at an interval of thirty yards as he walked with rapid pace, looking neither to the right nor left. He walked down the Canebière, and made his way through the market place towards the Old Port and along the quayside. Through the cluster of masts we could see him approach a tall block of modern flats. He signalled us to stop, turned back and whispered to us in a shop doorway.

"I think there is someone watching the flat, hide yourselves here like a couple of good scouts till I give the signal."

We had to smile in spite of our dangerous position and hid in the doorway until we saw him lift his hat as a signal. We climbed to Maurice's flat on the fourth floor. The windows were open and a clean sea breeze filled large and comfortable rooms. Maurice hustled us into a spare bedroom and ordered us to put on heavy felt slippers. They were similar to those which Keitel wore in his cell at Nuremberg four years later, making him ridiculous and unmilitary. We wore our slippers all the time we were in the flat to deaden the sound of footfalls for the inmates of the flat below were suspected of being on the side of Vichy. Of the many British prisoners of war sheltered by Maurice and his wife, Claire, for several gallant months not one was caught in the flat.

In the living-room there was a window-seat, looking down over the Old Port, from which we could watch the shipping. We sat there one evening during a conference of the principal members of the escape organisation and I had further opportunity to study the men and women who did this secret and valiant work. They came to the flat, one by one, each giving a special knock on the door. First came René, an Englishman born in France, red-cheeked and handsome and about twenty-five years old. The next arrival was Solon. He was a Greek, middle-aged, suave and polite and obviously successful in business. His clothes were of the best Riviera style and he carried a mahogany stick and gloves. He had about him an air of authority and took the chair as if he was presiding at a board meeting. He received Woollatt and myself with great courtesy regretting the absence of the chief of the escape organisation who, he said mysteriously, was "abroad." He might have been discussing the absence of some social acquaintance from his haunts at Nice or Monte Carlo, so pleasantly remote from the grim reality was his conversation. Yet when the conference began, he spoke with a sense of command. He, too, was later decorated by the Allies for his splendid courage in rescuing soldiers and airmen.

Last of all came Timon. He was also a Greek, a tall olive-skinned person with a flaxen-haired wife. Timon was like his compatriot, a man of business, full of courage and resource. His wife puzzled me greatly. I watched her china-blue eyes as she listened to Solon announcing plans to convoy escaped prisoners to Spain. I did not hear her speak as the others debated among themselves.

When the conference was over Claire served drinks and coffee. Woollatt and I were asked about our adventures. Outside, the Old Port of Marseilles was calm and the sunset illuminated the window-seat on which we sat leaving the rest of the room in darkness.

"How did the Germans treat you?"

"Very badly," I said. "You see we really understand them."

"I wonder," came a soft voice from the darkness of the room.

To my surprise the discussion ended abruptly and the members of the escape organisation dispersed by torchlight.

"Why did Timon's wife speak like that?" I asked Maurice as we went to bed in the spare room.

"My dear fellow, she is a German and a Communist to boot. Do not drop the heavy brick. Cheers, you chaps."

He closed the door and, somewhat deflated, I crept to bed.

CHAPTER XI

A WHOLE week we stayed in Maurice's flat till René appeared one morning to take us to the station. While we stood in the booking-hall he took our tickets. I noticed that a blond young man in a beret stood gazing at us. He had an elderly companion, a small man with a grizzled moustache who stood vacantly holding a basketwork case. His eyes had a meaningless expression. The younger man approached me and asked for a light. I struck a rotten French match which spluttered in front of his Gauloise cigarette. He puffed for a moment and said in French:

"Where is René?"

I pretended not to understand.

"I can see you are English," said the young man, "because you did not say '*Il n'y a pas de quoi*' when I thanked you for the light."

I was annoyed and frightened; I turned away and motioned to Woollatt to follow. Then came René, with our tickets.

"This," he said, pointing to the two strangers, "is Mr. Roberts and Mr. Roberts, junior, who are to travel with you to Spain."

Hugh Woollatt and I, a little nettled by the ease with which Mr. Roberts, junior, had penetrated our disguise, bowed rigidly and walked to the train for Toulouse.

The Roberts, father and son, had made contact with the escape organisation on their arrival in Marseilles through one of its numerous intermediaries. Mr. Roberts, born in Liverpool, had been employed, so far as I could understand, by a firm in Paris which printed railway, bus and theatre tickets. A widower of sixty-five, he had an Irish passport. He had been interned by the Germans but released into the unoccupied zone, and now, with Roberts junior, aged eighteen, wished to get to England. Mr. Roberts, senior, did not seem to me an ideal companion for a journey through Vichy France and a crossing of the Pyrenees by night. He was frail and nervous and complaining. He had far too much luggage, one suitcase consisting entirely of religious books. When he spoke it was in a slow plaintive voice. His son, however, was a splendid young man whose aim was to join the Commandos when he reached England.

Soon we were crammed into a third-class carriage with hard wooden seats. Opposite, sat a gendarme on leave with his wife and four small children who climbed on our knees and plucked at the moustache of Mr. Roberts, senior. I was filled with exasperation and alarm. The corridor was so full of people that we could not enjoy the spring sunshine and watch the Mediterranean flowers through the windows. We passed through Tarascon and Nîmes where I occasionally glimpsed green fields and gaily-coloured villages. It was hot and the gendarme fell asleep, paying little attention to us or our unusual clothes. Once, he gave me a prodigious wink, apropos of nothing.

Our arrival at Toulouse in the early afternoon coincided with the inspection of a French Airforce guard of honour at the station. A superior officer in pointed black boots stepped up and down before each rank to the accompaniment of murmurs of admiration from the women gathered outside the station. Who this grand personage was I do not know nor how it was that Vichy France maintained an airforce in the neighbourhood of Toulouse. We were stopped by gendarmes at the exit and told to wait with other passengers in the booking hall. From the window we could see this comedy as we fretted anxiously for over fifteen minutes. All around us were the searching eyes of a large force of gendarmes. There was a sigh of relief among the passengers from the train as the parade was dismissed. A roll of drums and a feeble bugle-call ushered the Personage from the forecourt of the station to his waiting car. There was a furious rush of passengers, sweeping the gendarmes from the main entrance. In the confusion our Czech papers were never examined at the exit, so we hurried into the town.

In a few minutes Woollatt and I had joined with René

and the Roberts's at the Hotel de Paris. It was old and sinister with a courtyard and an interior gallery on the first floor which led to moth-eaten bedrooms. Here we had to stay for a week with mounting impatience. By day, we were obliged to go into the town to eat sparse meals for which we had to surrender forged coupons. After we had eaten, we would return on the orders of René, to pace a large half-furnished, double bedroom listening to voices speaking in many languages on the other side of the walls. Poles, Frenchmen, Scotsmen and Australians, all fugitives from the Germans, assembling at the hotel to prepare for the journey to Spain. The authorities of Toulouse believing the hotel to be practically empty never inspected the rooms on the upper floors. Indeed ordinary visitors were seldom admitted and the gendarme who inspected the register each evening found nothing unusual.

Every man received from René a new set of papers. We were given with our Czech identity cards, forged instructions to report to the centre for refugees, the *centre d'acueil* at Banyuls-sur-Mer near the Spanish frontier and close to Port Vendres.

Six days later, a party of twelve escapers including Hugh Woollatt and I left Toulouse by the early morning train for Perpignan. They were travelling in parties of two in different sections of the train. Some were Poles, two were Canadian priests and Woollatt and I, the only two British travelled together. We changed at Narbonne. The Perpignan train would not be in for some hours so we walked into the town carrying new suitcases. A sharp-eyed gendarme evidently scenting the Black Market, studied us acutely as we left the railway station. He followed us all the way through the town until we entered a café and lost sight of him.

"Don't get drunk," said Woollatt.

"Why not?" said I.

"You look so appallingly suspicious when you do," said Woollatt.

"So do you."

After this we sat sulking in the café, drinking an occasional cognac until it was time to return to the railway station where we boarded the train for Perpignan. As it drew into the station I saw René in one of the carriages, but carefully avoiding him, entered a carriage with an old peasant woman.

The hot Mediterranean sun beat upon the carriage raising the smell of varnish and causing the wooden seats to crack. The train passed beside large blue lakes on its way to Perpignan. A soft haze hung over the distant ocean and Woollatt and the old woman slumbered in the lazy air. I lay back and closed my eyes and wondered if this was to be the end of my journey. There were several jumps ahead but this fierce race across one half of Europe was drawing near the finish. A frightful exhaustion came over me like the last heartbreaking lap of a half-mile race when breath comes to the runner only in pain.

Perpignan, Argèles, Collioure. The train stopped at each station in the brazen sunlight, taking its time and prolonging our suspense. The old woman left and new passengers carrying market produce entered the carriage. We were forced to sit in silence watching the stations while the passengers studied and then sank into sleep as the train sped towards Port Vendres beside the shimmering sea.

We leapt to the platform at Port Vendres and soon mingled with the crowd forcing its way towards the exit. I was on the edge of the throng, separated from the remainder of René's party. The crowd pushed its way past a single gendarme who vainly tried to examine each passport. Then his sharp eyes alighted on me and selected me for special surveillance. I knew that there was a guilty expression on my face. He restrained me gently with his hand, as if I were a schoolboy without a ticket, until the station was nearly clear of travellers, then examined my papers, and demanded:

"Where are you going?"

"To the *Centre d'Accueil* for refugees."

"Are you British?"

"No, Czech."

'Well, good luck anyway!" he said.

He released me. I walked anxiously to the waterfront where young girls and boys were walking in the evening glow among the many-coloured boats. By the seashore I found the Poles and Canadian priests white-faced and anxious thinking I had been detained. I now felt safe from gendarmes and reassured them confidently. Then:

"Look!" said René, pointing towards the station.

A gendarme was riding down the hill from the station towards the waterfront, his bicycle throwing up clouds of dust. Behind him came two more ominous figures on bicycles. Our group of fugitives stood undecided on the shingle.

"Meet at José's house," shouted René, as he started to run. We knew that he was referring to an emergency address given to us in Toulouse.

We tore across the sands, leaping over anchors, rocks and pieces of wreckage, scattering towards the brushwood in the low hills at the foot of the mountains. I wondered as I ran what was to become of old Mr. Roberts and Mr. Roberts, junior, and then remembered that both had Irish passports and spoke perfect French. It was we, the British and Polish, men of military age for whom the gendarmes were specially searching, and Vichy prison camps awaited us if we were caught. There was a faint derisive cheer from the people on the waterfront as we disappeared towards the hills. I did not see the gendarmes but they must have soon given up the chase for there was no sound of pursuit.

Woollatt and I, whistling to each other, soon made contact in the brushwood beyond the last row of white houses. We stood among stunted trees where we could scan the town and watch the sun sink beyond the sea.

There came a crashing in the bushes behind us. The familiar face of Jan, a Polish sergeant, who had been with us at Toulouse, appeared grinning. He was trying to find the way to José's house.

When all was quiet below and darkness had embraced the town, the three of us crept to a white house standing on its own at the foot of the hill and soon identified it as José's house by the muffled sound of English voices within. Three knocks on the door and a tall, rather pretty French woman softly bade us enter. She had a good-humoured voice and a strong energetic face. I did not hear her name mentioned. The house was in darkness save for candles in two rooms. Gradually, I was able to discern familiar faces. René, the two Roberts, the two Canadian priests and the Poles were safe and sound. Only one of the Polish officers was missing. They were seated round a green baize table drinking rum and eating a last meal of sandwiches before the journey over the mountains. Everyone was talking excitedly of their escape from the gendarmes. The Roberts's and René had not been questioned owing to their berets and French appearance. The woman bustled round the house preparing food and served us each with a bowl of warm soup.

A little dark man dressed in the costume of a guide and wearing pure white boots now took his place at the table. He began by asking briskly in a mixture of French and Spanish for money, and large quantities of notes in bundles were taken from money belts or unpicked from the lining of coats and placed before him as if he were a croupier at a Casino. René supplied the money for most of his party, but the Roberts's paid their own passage. The funds for our journey had been entrusted to René by Solon in Marseilles. I looked at the notes, mysterious in their crisp new bundles under the candlelight and wondered where they came from. José, the guide, collected the bundles and counted the notes with care. He appeared satisfied with his payment for he handed them to the woman who vanished into the darkness of the house.

José was a determined character, thin and wiry, and his eyes were always watchful. His face was the colour of a walnut and deeply lined. When he laughed his teeth showed very white in the candlelight. He earned his living by smuggling. The war had brought him great prosperity on account of the valuable cargoes of spies and escapers requiring safe passage over the Pyrenees.

When the money had been taken away, José said he must inspect the belongings of all those who intended to cross the mountains. Woollatt and I stuffed our pockets with dry socks and packets of chocolate and left our suitcases in the house. The others were asked to discard all unnecessary possessions. Poor old Mr. Roberts vainly pleaded to be allowed to take his suitcase of bibles and devotional books. José was adamant and the holy books were left behind. His other suitcase of clothes Mr. Roberts insisted on taking, much to our consternation for it was heavy and the weather in the mountains promised to be stormy.

At midnight we shook hands with the staunch René. José opened the door gently and, one by one, we stepped on to a path which led to the hills. The night was clear and starlit, but deep clouds moved threateningly towards us over the Mediterranean. I could see the mountains dark and formidable as we began to climb the foothills. For me they were the last barrier but one to cross. In that cold air, as I climbed the path, listening to the others struggling among the steep banks of scrub and the sound of boots now on chalk, now on flint, I steeled myself to meet new dangers. At that stage of the war, the Fascist Government of Spain might have found British officers useful pawns in the game with Hitler. Not till I reached the Rock of Gibraltar would I be safe from the enemy.

José's white boots in front of us stood out clearly as we climbed with him to a height of 1,000 feet and then stopped for a short rest. It was three in the morning and we could see the clouds advancing from the sea behind us. I stood and drank from a small flask of brandy and turned to look towards the heights above. Around me, the remainder of the party lay panting and whispering to each other on the peaty turf. The path continued up slopes of heather. Then came slippery shale and stones. We pulled ourselves from tuft to tuft and then clambered among rocks where icy streams flowed. Slipping backwards and sometimes falling in the darkness, we began to feel our energy draining from us.

At four o'clock we rested again beneath a sharp face of rock. My breath came in painful gasps and I felt my heart would burst. Woollatt and I were young and fit after many adventures, yet we were badly exhausted. The two Canadian priests, spare and ascetic, and the Poles, lay panting and helpless, Mr. Roberts, comforted by his son, was groaning. He had begun to fear that he would be left to die among the mountains. He complained miserably in a mixture of Irish and French. José, unmoved by the climb, silenced him with heartless laughter. In half an hour we moved again towards the summit, lifting frail old Mr. Roberts like a parcel from man to man, hoisting him by his arms and legs. Some of us cursing and panting took turns at carrying his heavy suitcase.

Daybreak found us among black rocks near the summit eating a breakfast of cheese and hard-boiled eggs and drinking brandy. I had time to study our party in the grey light. The priests reticent and pale, the Poles talkative and full of suggestions. Hugh Woollatt stood with his long dark lock of hair hanging below his beret.

Then suddenly a storm descended on the mountain like a great bird with outstretched wings. Soon everything was drenched in fine rain. The wind blew so that we could hardly stand upright. Above and around us were only the rain clouds and the desolate mountains. In this misery and confusion old Mr. Roberts' suitcase was by general consent hurled among the rocks. There was a feeble round of applause but the old man was near to tears.

For many hours the rain lashed us with pitiless force. The mountain paths filled with water holes as we splashed through the mist, dragging the old man till he could walk no more. The youngest of us, Woollatt, Roberts junr. and I, took it in turns to carry him on our shoulders. Once, when he was on my back he seemed to be unconscious and swayed from side to side. Only with great difficulty could I maintain my balance among the wet rocks.

There was a moment when we had to consider whether we should leave him in some farm-house but he cried so piteously that we had not the heart to leave him.

At noon, the rains ceased as suddenly as they had come, leaving only a blank fog as we began to descend the mountain on the Spanish side, along shepherd tracks in the direction of the town of Jonqueras. In an hour the sun shone and we were on level ground. Mr. Roberts was just able to stumble along with us among farms and wide green pastures. We headed away from Jonqueras towards the railway which, crossing the frontier at Cerbère, led to Figueras. All that day we tramped heavily through wet fields and along tracks, sometimes carrying Mr. Roberts, sometimes helping him to walk. Once we nearly ran into frontier guards. "That way is no bon," said José laconically, leading us out of their sight. I caught a glimpse of light green uniforms and black cocked hats in a valley.

And so we marched on in a drawn-out column crossing the river Muga and trudging through fields, heading towards the railway. As the sun set we were among small villages and ploughed fields. Every one of us was exhausted. Several times it seemed impossible to carry the old man any more and he was left to walk far behind in the dusk calling to us. And then, realising his danger, we would go back and pick him up again.

The end of the journey came quickly. In the darkness we crouched beside a roughly plastered wall in a Spanish village, waiting for the signal to advance and then, still following the white boots of José, we reached the railway panting and cursing in our exhaustion. We came to a rough wooden platform and a faint light showed from a shed. In its doorway was the stout figure of a man who stood aside as we blundered into the shed and flung ourselves on narrow bunks.

When I had recovered a little I rose to examine with interest the stout man who welcomed us. He was dressed in a smart pale grey suit with a pearl in his tie and wore a hat at a rakish angle. There came from him a strong Parisian scent and I could see his fat white hands, carefully manicured adorned with rings. He looked at us humorously through his thick black-rimmed glasses and said in broken English: 'Welcome to Spain, gentlemen. Rest yourselves. It is now one o'clock and the train for Barcelona arrives at six."

Old Mr. Roberts did not hear him for he was unconscious in his wooden bunk.

CHAPTER XII

THERE was no time to dry our clothes. We took off our boots and socks and shook and squeezed the water from them on the floor. Then we said good-bye to José. He shook hands, saying briefly that he must be under the cover of the hills before dawn. This wiry little man showed no signs of an ordeal which had lasted nearly a day and a night. The door opened shedding a ray of light over the field beside the railway line as he went out into the night. I followed his white boots for some distance into the darkness until the fat man closed the door of the shed.

Woollatt and I alone were awake. The fat man whose name we discovered was Pedro was leaning against a table. He offered us cigarettes. The smoke rose up into the shadows of the roof as we sat at the table in the light of the railway lamp. Pedro watched us through his glasses in silence. I could see the powder on his round white cheeks and chin.

While the others slept we talked to him, and he took from his pocket a flask of Spanish brandy. He leaned towards us offering the flask. His sophisticated perfume, mingled oddly with the smell of damp clothes and socks and boots. Around us our companions snored noisily. I took the flask and listened to his boasting talk. His beady black eyes sharply reflected the lamplight.

"A German steamer at Barcelona, she blew up—pouf! That was last week. Very extraordinary!" He said in a strange lisping French.

"Who blew it up?"

"Friends of mine. It was a good show and worth the money."

He made a little gesture with his hand to indicate the passing of notes between his fingers. "In war," he spoke greedily, "one can do business with one's friends."

"Where are you taking us?" said Woollatt.

"To the British in Barcelona. I have friends among the police who control the train. You shall see. It is always dangerous to be without friends in wartime."

"Sometimes it is difficult to know who are your friends," I said, still fearful of agents provocateurs.

The fat man turned and stared at me. He leaned forward for a moment. He seemed a little annoyed, then smiled effusively.

"Money talks," he said, and then repeated the phrase several times as if to reassure himself.

I did not like the little fellow nor did he like me. His eyes narrowed a little fiercely.

"I shall have a look round outside," he said, "the train arrives at six o'clock."

Pedro opened the door and went out.

"You be careful," said Woollatt, "I don't trust these Spaniards."

"This man will do anything for money. He doesn't care who he works for."

We lay down in our wet clothes to sleep.

The cold air of the mountains blew into the shed at dawn and there came the rumbling of a train. Never have I seen such a ragamuffin crew as we were as we boarded it. All of us were grey and tired. Our clothes and boots were caked with clay and mud. We took our places in a long, first-class compartment with seats each side of a corridor and promptly fell asleep. The train, stopping at numerous stations, collected smart business men in black suits with pointed shoes and pearl tie-pins travelling to Barcelona. They read their newspapers without the least concern.

A tall, hawk-like person with a trim moustache, dressed in a dark brown suit and hat, walked between the rows of seats, drawing back the lapel of his coat to show a shining, five-starred police badge. Walking beside him in a mincing fashion came Pedro, pointing out his "friends," tired, dejected tramps, dozing in the early morning sun. The hawk-like detective smiled with a twist of his lips, and glaring fiercely at the business men, demanded their identity cards. The business men, accustomed to living in a Police State, took it all as a matter of course, and smiled knowingly to themselves, smoothing their sleek hair and adjusting their tie-pins. I wondered what was in their minds. Here were twelve persons who had entered Spain illegally, showing every sign of their recent arrival and travelling quite openly on an early morning train to Barcelona. Pedro and the detective made no attempt to conceal the joke.

Towards eight in the morning the train, high-powered and smooth, ran into Barcelona. We walked, still dazed with sleep to the exits of the station, confused by bright colours and sounds. The sun shone through high, cathedral-like windows on to the platforms. Formidable police stood at each doorway ready to pounce on us, but Pedro laughingly drawing their attention to us, marched us as if we were a party of schoolchildren, into the warm air. Scarlet flowers bloomed in the gardens outside the station, and along the sidewalks of the streets men and women wearing dark glasses, walked to their work. Beside a saffron-coloured block of workmen's dwellings stood an old car. Its driver was a young Englishman from the British Consulate with a military moustache and a green felt hat. He told Woollatt, the two Roberts and me to get inside, and requested Pedro to buy tram tickets for the others. My last glimpse of Pedro showed him shepherding the Poles across the street. Years afterwards I heard that he was working for both sides taking money from British and Germans alike. I believe that Franco had him shot.

The car, driven rapidly over the tram lines, stopped at a small modern café. We followed the young man in the green hat inside and sat down to a breakfast of rolls and coffee. The warm coffee with cream and rolls dispelled the damp misery of the past two nights. Straightening his Royal Artillery tie, the Englishman from the Consulate asked for the bill and led us back to his car. On the other side of the road a music-hall Spanish detective stroked his pointed black beard as he stood in a shop doorway recording the number of the car. The Englishman took the wheel of the car and showed no concern about the detective. He explained to us with mock solemnity that in a police state such things were to be expected. I found no comfort in his blasé attitude, for in the last two years I had had experience of secret police and I did not feel they were a subject for frivolity. As the car came to a standstill outside the British Consulate we saw two more Spanish detectives lounging against a tree, watching our arrival with ill-concealed interest.

Medical attention was quickly procured for Mr. Roberts, but apart from him our weather-beaten party raised no consternation among the Consular staff. They recorded our particulars, provided us with Spanish suits of greenish-blue tweed, and then distributed us by taxi to billets in obscure parts of the town.

Woollatt and I spent several days hiding in a Spanish workman's house in the suburbs, visited occasionally by a pretty Englishwoman from the Consulate, who listened patiently to our loud demands to be taken to Gibraltar at once. The Spaniard and his wife with whom we lived were honest Catalans hostile to Franco, who seemed to live almost entirely on fish. Their kitchen where we sat by day was always stifling. We were not allowed to leave the house, for fear of being seen by Franco's spies or prying neighbours, except to walk through a dark backyard to a wooden convenience. I paid more visits to this place than were necessary, driven into the yard by the stench of the kitchen. Our food was brought from the Consulate and cooked by the Spanish woman. But I had little appetite. Each evening she ate her plate of fish, crushing the heads with her teeth. The sickening crackle made me feel sick.

"I don't understand," said Woollatt provocatively, "why you are so squeamish."

"It must be the return to civilisation. I ate a piece of cat when I was in Germany," I said.

Early in the morning of the first of May, 1942, a large Bentley drew up outside the house with two men inside and Woollatt and I, dressed in our blue-green Spanish suits got into it. We said good-bye to our Spanish hosts as day began to dawn. Huddled in the back seat of the Bentley, I wondered at the identity of our companions. Both of them were tall and handsome, wearing discreet check suits in the best Foreign Office style. Their soft brown hats were bent at a becoming angle. As it grew light and the Bentley hummed its way over the long dusty road to Madrid, I could see their well-kept hands. Despite the fact that they took not the slightest notice of either of their passengers, I felt for the first time in those long, dangerous months that I was home.

But the danger was not over. I was still a refugee from Hitler, an escaped prisoner of war, with no status in a neutral country. My authority for being in Spain did not exist, and in those days diplomatic plates on a car were of limited protection. We stopped half-way to Madrid beside the long, white, dusty road, to eat a picnic lunch and drink red wine from bottles. In the hot sun the Foreign Office officials took off their coats and old-school ties and laid them on the seats of the car. They were obviously apprehensive of the car being searched. The road was straight and clouds of dust warned us of the approach of other vehicles. Several times during the picnic Woollatt and I, leaving our sandwiches, had to take to low hills beside the road, and hide until the cars were past. From behind a cluster of huge stones we could see the diplomats eating hard-boiled eggs as they paced languidly in the sun.

We got back into the Bentley and the sparse Spanish countryside swept by. In the evening we came to the outskirts of Madrid, then sped through the streets to the British Embassy. Through a high gateway we walked, into a garden full of flowers where the Assistant Military Attaché received us in forbidding fashion threatening appalling penalties if we said a word to anyone of our adventures. I was anxious to meet someone to whom I could talk in confidence. This official apparently regarded all escapers as diplomatic embarrassments and ignored the fact that we possessed useful information.

We entered a hall and ascended wide stairs to the room above, where the First Secretary of the Embassy sat. He rose to meet us, a big man with a welcoming handshake. He was not paralysed by bureaucratic caution or embarrassed by diplomacy, but human and kind. The contrast made a deep impression upon me. I told him of Alex and Pierre and Maurice and their demand that they should be allowed to send more young men of the Allies ready to fight, and fewer elderly civilians over the mountains to Spain. I asked him to send a message on the B.B.C. announcing our safe arrival. He grimaced.

"It can't be done. There are so many messages already."

"But—I was thinking of Mademoiselle Jeanne at Annemass."

"They will hear by other means."

"What other means?"

"What you need is a drink. Come with me."

We followed him to a large wooden building in the Embassy garden, where twenty or thirty men were drinking beer and sherry. They came from every Allied nation, all of them tough, hard and determined, all of them ready to fight. They were impressive people, gay and easy to talk to, these successful escapists. I heard my name spoken, and turned to see the familiar face of Major Philip Newman, D.S.O., M.C., of the Royal Army Medical Corps. Here was another strange coincidence, like the meeting with Dr. von Erlach, in Switzerland. Philip Newman had lived before the war at Ingatestone, near to my parents' home in Essex, and our next meeting was in the camp at Spangenburg in 1940. He was moved with the wounded, due for repatriation to England, to a hospital in France and from there escaped over the Pyrenees to Spain, arriving shortly before I did. Thus did we meet reaching Madrid by different routes. We remained together for the rest of the journey to England, and returned to our homes near Ingatestone by the same train.

I slept that night in great happiness. At eight in the morning the Bishop of Gibraltar held a short communion service before our departure from the Embassy. Those who had come through to safety were deeply moved. Then we said good-bye to the Embassy officials with regret. Every man who passed through this strange wooden building on his way to freedom during the years of the war will remember the Ambassador, Lord Templewood, and most of his staff with gratitude.

After breakfast, we rushed like schoolboys to a large orange motor-coach driven by a small grinning Gibraltarian with a chauffeur's cap. Mysteriously we were described on the documents we carried as students under the charge of old Mr. Roberts, now recovered from his journey, and who alone was above military age and safe from arrest. The Gibraltarian announced amid cheers that no one was to get drunk or speak to any Spaniard, and then, still grinning trod on the accelerator, and drove the coach at breakneck speed away from Madrid.

We shouted and laughed in several languages, as the coach crossed the Tagus and climbed through the mountains beside the deep gorges. Some of these tough men, in their excitement, bounced up and down in their seats like little children.

We spent the night in a hotel at Cordoba under strict surveillance from the secret police, who entered the hotel frequently to scrutinise our bogus signatures in the register. In the lounge we drank wine and sherry till a late hour talking over our adventures. Officers and men alike, we were united in a sense of great achievement. Even old Mr. Roberts had recovered from his ordeal and began to talk of his life in the internment camp where the Germans had sent him before his release to the unoccupied zone. The terror and discomfort seemed to melt away as the night wore on. Each man spoke of what he would do first on arrival in England.

"I shall sink three pints of mild and bitter," said one.

"I shall take my girl for a drive on the Downs," said another.

There was nothing spiritual in their ecstasies. They felt that for their efforts the world owed them the women and the beer they had missed during their years of imprisonment.

Next morning the motor-coach set off for Malaga, its passengers subdued by the debauches of the night before, but the brisk air of the mountains soothed our headaches, and we came to a restaurant beside the seashore at Malaga where mellow wines restored our joy of yesterday. The grinning chauffeur paid for the meals, supervised by the senior officer of the party. Then to the accompaniment of carefree songs and laughter, the orange coach careered along the twisting roads to Gibraltar. It was the gayest party I could remember since the day when the second eleven returned after a victory over a detestable rival, fifteen years before.

The Rock showed itself before we reached La Linea as a dark shadow against the clouds. Slowly it took shape as we passed over the flat country before the frontier, and watched aircraft and shipping in the Bay. At the gateway of La Linea, Spanish frontier guards argued cynically about our papers and demanded our signatures. They were not impressed by our thinly-veiled identity, but the afternoon was hot, and with angry resignation they stamped our papers and let the coach proceed.

It is a frequent occurrence in life that an event most keenly awaited ends in a pitiful anti-climax. My return to British territory, the end of my escapes, and, so it had seemed to me, the whole glorious achievement, was no more dramatic than the arrival of an unexpected recruit in barracks. The secrecy surrounding our movements did not, of course, permit of a red carpet and a fanfare of trumpets. But we had, owing to some misunderstanding, not even been heard of by the Military authorities, accustomed as they were to the frequent arrival of mysterious travellers at La Linea. An hour passed as we stamped our feet outside an orderly-room guarded severely by two Red Caps in case, apparently, we should escape back to Spain.

This is the kind of expert refrigeration of the emotions in which most British institutions, especially the Army, specialise to a high degree. As I watched aircraft take off along the runway of the newly constructed aerodrome into the white haze over the sea, I could not but resign myself to laughter. In that moment all my joy in reaching the Promised Land evaporated in the fug of the orderly-room, where pale clerks in shorts took our particulars and told us to wait outside.

Next came an Intelligence Officer, who remarked that it was Saturday afternoon—Saturday afternoon! Fancy escaping from Germany and arriving in a British fortress on Saturday afternoon! I remarked to Woollatt with simulated embarrassment that we had called on the wrong day. Saturday afternoon is, if anything, more sacred than Sunday, and no one but a fool who knows no better would time an escape to end in such a way. I tender this advice to future students of escaping in the unhappy event of another war.

Despite the week-end the Intelligence Officer was, nevertheless, human. He examined our documents, asked a few questions, and accompanied us by truck to be examined by the Medical Officer, who was out. A perfunctory inspection by a R.A.M.C. sergeant followed with the usual emphasis on lice and venereal disease. Then the officers were separated from the other ranks, a parting which filled me and indeed all of us with real regret. It is not possible to survive misfortune and adventure in several countries, to cross the Pyrenees, and travel on a sort of school outing through Spain, to be concerned whether a man is an officer or not.

Newman, Woollatt and I walked eagerly through the narrow streets of Gibraltar. I still wore my depressing Spanish suit. The trousers were too long and the coat too short. Sailors, soldiers, and airmen in shorts and shirt sleeves walked in groups, gazing at the tawdry merchandise in the shops and drinking in the cafés open to the street where raucous dance bands played. It was very hot as we entered a bar and began to drink pink gins. Across the street I could hear the loud earthy laughter of sailors as they purchased underclothes for their girls. Their red young faces glistened among the raffish heaps of blue and pink and black material revealingly demonstrated by a Spanish shop girl. I drank the second pink gin and joined in their laughter so that the sailors heard and waved cheerfully in my direction. I was thinking of a snowy day in January of the same year, fifteen hundred miles away in Leipzig when Luteyn and I, sheltering from the cold in a big store watched the hard, lascivious faces of the Nazis as they walked with their girl friends.

I ordered a third pink gin and the band in the café next door struck up "J'attendrai," murdering the melody. The music blared forth into the thronged street. Newman, Woollatt and I walked away towards the harbour, jostled by the noisy crowds of young men, and stood for a moment looking over the Bay. The moon had risen and the Rock stood above us half in the shadows, half aglow. Battleships, cruisers, aircraft carriers and other shipping lay serene and formidable. Near us the crew of an anti-aircraft gun were drinking tea in the moonlight. None of us spoke. I was wondering how many years would pass before I could feel part of this light-hearted world of soldiers and sailors.

A prosaic nature of my return to the jurisdiction of the Army led me to exaggerate its apparent lack of humanity. Next day I found myself in an officers' mess where I sat in my Spanish suit reading the *Illustrated London News*. At one o'clock a crowd of young officers in khaki shorts bronzed and happy burst into the room. It was not long before they drew me into conversation and plied me with pints of beer so that I began to talk eloquently of my journey over Europe. They listened to me with interest. As soon as I reached a point in the narrative which seemed confidential I tried to change the subject.

I felt the eyes of the Intelligence Officer in the small of my back. I knew he was coming towards me. He edged his way into the circle of young officers listening to me as they held up their beer mugs. The sweat glistened on my forehead. The Intelligence Officer watched me sharply behind his hornrimmed spectacles. If he thought at that moment that he bore any resemblance to the Gestapo I could have told him a different story. I could have told him things that no one except an Intelligence Officer, apparently, was supposed to know; about a pale cruel man in the Gestapo office at Plock and a Polish woman with bare feet who was not afraid to die.

I found myself making the officers laugh with a story about an Englishman who threw a roll of bread at an Italian diplomat in a restaurant in Switzerland. The sweat ran down their cheeks as they listened. The Intelligence Officer sat next to me at lunch. "You are a good conversationalist, I perceive," he said in a high-pitched academic voice. "I hope you will be careful not to say too much." I beamed at him. It seemed like receiving a school report which was better than one hoped.

After two days the escapers received orders to board the troopship for the journey home. As we climbed aboard, an official of the Foreign Office met us and arranged to send messages to our families. Clad in a battledress without badges of rank I felt incongruous. I carried a new suitcase and I still wore the same brown Army boots I had worn when I was captured at Calais.

The troopship went her way in fine weather. Once, a U-boat returning to its base caused an alarm. The men stood in three ranks on the boat deck, with their lifejackets. When the danger was over they dispersed, aimlessly, round the ship. The officers, landlubbers, sat drinking in the saloon exchanging endless yarns and making nervous jokes about the "tin fish." The "tin fish" was for me a symbol. It represented one more unpredictable obstacle in the race home. I waited for it every night but it never came. I was more fortunate than one of the escapers who followed me in a later party. Captain Barry O'Sullivan, M.C., of the Royal Tank Regiment who accepted a berth in the sloop *Wild Swan*, was sunk in the Bay of Biscay and spent some hours in the water before he was rescued. He had escaped in 1941 from Hugh Woollatt's camp at Biberach.

Interminably, the troopship ploughed through the Atlantic seeking to avoid U-boats until one cloudy morning a Sunderland circled, firing a recognition signal. There was a murmur of relief. A day passed and we were in the fog of the Clyde, waiting to disembark. Alongside, a huge liner, packed to the brim with American troops, moved slowly up the river. It was hard for me to grasp, I who had been reading Charlotte Brontë in the town gaol of Colditz on the night of Pearl Harbor.

The escaped prisoners were permitted to land in advance and received orders to travel by train to Glasgow. I clambered with the others into a launch and landed on the quay at Gourock at noon on the 13th May, 1942. My first sensation was of extreme depression. All along the Clyde baleful clouds of mist obscured the shipping. And in Gourock among the bleak houses there seemed no ray of welcome, no familiar sign. We had to wait for the train, so Philip Newman led us along deserted streets until we came to a dreary pub where, without elation we performed the ceremony of drinking our first pint of beer in Britain. Someone asked for a ham sandwich. There was a shocked silence. A broad grin broke over the face of a sallow Scotswoman and her laughter was like the wail of a banshee. We edged our way out of the pub, disconsolate and embarrassed, unable to recapture the old world or understand the new, and loafed about the streets until the train for Glasgow was due to depart.

Hours later we sat, escapers of all ranks, at a round table in a Glasgow hotel, waiting to catch the night train to London. I was dizzy with tiredness and its effort of trying to adjust myself to these surroundings was intense. I saw people in the restaurant as in a vision. Suddenly the vision turned to reality. A girl came into the restaurant. It was my younger sister Rosamund.

At first I could not grasp that she was not some echo of the past, some hallucination. I was like Dante confronted with the spirit of Beatrice. I remained at the table refusing to believe that this was she. She came closer and when there could be no further doubt I rushed to meet her.

So far as I knew our movements were shrouded in the deepest secrecy. What was she doing in Glasgow?

"Did you know I was coming?" I explained.

"I had no idea at all. The last I heard of you was at the Hotel Suisse in Fribourg." She was as overcome as I was.

"Didn't you know we had reached Gibraltar?"

"I had no news at all."

"How do you come to be in Glasgow? This is the strangest coincidence of all."

"I have been on holiday up here for ten days. I am going back to London tonight on the 10.30."

"So are we. There is something extraordinary about these meetings. It has been happening all the way from Germany."

I told her of the meeting in Dr. von Erlach's surgery, of my reunion with Philip Newman in Madrid.

It seemed that Fate had specially placed these friends at different stages on my journey to help me on my way. Then there had been the wicket-gate in the moat-bridge which pointed the way to freedom like a ford across a difficult river. These things had brought me to the hotel in Glasgow where I sat between my sister and a tough little corporal who had escaped single-handed from the enemy.

When the train was due to leave the whole party entered the station at Glasgow. At the barrier a furious scene occurred before the train left. The tough little corporal had, owing to some clerical error, been omitted from the warrant on which we were to travel. Newman, Woollatt and I argued with the Military Police. The other N.C.O.s who had escaped and Rosamund joined in. When the argument was at its height, a thin drooping full Colonel in a British warm, the picture of bureaucratic gloom, intervened. We resolved that the corporal was not to be left behind. The military bureaucrat thought otherwise and supported the minor bureaucrats at the barrier.

"If this man is left here I shall see to it that the War Office is informed of this scandal," said I, wildly, to the colonel. "Surely you can accept the word of officers who have escaped from Germany."

The white lips of the colonel moved in a dyspeptic grimace.

"I do not know you," he said to us. "You may be German agents."

There was impatient laughter. The guard blew his whistle and we rushed past the barrier dragging the corporal with us. The officials stood stock still in outraged dignity but they did not attempt to restrain us. Even Hitler had not been able to do that.

CHAPTER XIII

THE express from Glasgow drew into Euston on the morning of May 14th, 1942. I sat in the carriage waiting till all the passengers had left so that I could savour the thrill of being once more in the familiar station. The leather buttons on the upholstery, the handle of the heat regulator, women in tweeds from the country loudly summoning porters from the open windows, all gave me intense pleasure. Home again! I could see a row of London taxis moving slowly towards the queue of travellers. The sunlight filtered through the roof. Bright patches shone on the platform before the bookstalls. I looked through the window in happy reverie.

There was the sound of ammunition boots on the platform and a naïve face peered into the compartment. It belonged to a very young military policeman. The skin of his face was burnished like a bright saucepan. He eyed me awkwardly. The Colonel's messenger I thought. Was I to be arrested as a German agent and marched to Wormwood

Scrubs? I began to conjure up visions of a new prison, a fresh period of confinement. I looked round the carriage for a means of escape. Should I leave the train, then dash across the platform among the taxi queue? There was no basic difference between this station and the stations at Posen, at Dresden and Leipzig. The problem was the same, to know when to make a dash for it.

The military policeman continued to stare into the carriage. My battledress without badges of rank, worn with a white shirt and khaki tie puzzled him. He straightened himself and recovered sufficiently to make a very creditable salute.

"Sir?" he said inquiringly.

"Yes."

"Have you escaped?"

"I hope so."

"Major Newman's compliments, Sir, but the party have gone to the hotel for breakfast."

I grinned at him and his bright face took on the shade of a setting sun. I took down my suitcase and walked towards the barrier. Beyond it, my sister who had travelled in a sleeper was waiting for me.

We walked outside threading our way among the hurrying crowd of office workers. This moment of awakening was painful. I was like a man recovering consciousness, fighting within his mind to discover if he is in Life or Death. The mists recede and he sees the dentist bending over him advancing as if to strike once more. He yells and the mists vanish revealing the apologetic dentist and a nurse holding a kidney dish.

There was a War Reserve constable directing the traffic at the entrance to the station. He was an old man with a large waxed moustache wearing the Mons Star. He had a face like a photograph I remembered of some victim of the 1918 retreat, fading in the shadows of a country cottage in Essex. It seemed that he looked at me in no friendly manner as if I were a suspected person loitering with intent to commit a felony.

I began to realise my exaggerated fears were the result of months of pursuit and suspicion. I hurried with my sister to the hotel and up the steps. Nothing had changed except the bustle of khaki and an indefinable atmosphere which everyone called austerity. I laughed as I washed in the cloak-room with the other ex-prisoners. Austerity would not worry me. I had for long wondered whether Dr. Goebbels was correct in telling us that England was nearly starving.

The waiter advanced towards our table with a bleak expression. After the *débâcle* of the ham sandwich at Gourock I did not know what to order without incurring ridicule. The wailing laugh of the old Scotswoman in the pub still rang in my ears. My sister came to the rescue. There were corn-flakes and porridge; kipper and haddock; toast with the consistency of flannel. There is nothing which can bring a man, after long wandering, back to earth so swiftly as breakfast in a British railway hotel.

After breakfast I went with Newman and the others to be interrogated. Our taxi drew up before the entrance to the old Great Central Hotel at Marylebone, requisitioned as a transit camp for London District. The vehicle was old and wheezing like its driver who looked mournfully at us. He had two wisps of tobacco-stained moustache above his long mouth. He viewed our high-spirited party with irritation unable to respond to our mood. His glumness turned to loud abuse. We had no money for the fare!

"Nah then, you blinkin' aristocrats, wait till we have a Labour Government! That'll teach you to go riding round on kebs without paying."

I laughed heartily at the old man for I was in shabby battledress from Gibraltar. I was an aristocrat returning from a Continental tour of two years' duration. The taxi-man seemed to understand the futility of the class war.

"It's them bombs, sir. Awful it was. My old woman she never got over it. And here I was driving down through the city one night when one came down and blew the old keb right across the road. There was a poor young couple with me. I never saw 'em again. Never saw 'em again. I woke up in the 'ospital and they said they was both killed. I was lucky. Makes you a bit ratty nah and then though."

"Do they come over often now?"

"Why bless you no. We 'aven't 'ad no raids for months. Sometimes we 'ave one or two over. Nothing to worry about."

"I've been away a long time, you see."

Woollatt produced the money from some mysterious

source. The taximan's face resumed its normal expression. The gears emitted a grating noise and the old "keb" drew off unsteadily in the light morning rain.

I walked up the steps into the well-remembered hall of the Great Central Hotel with its Victorian figures in marble. The receptionists and waiters were gone and in their place military policemen and orderlies awaited me. I did not expect a red carpet for a returned prisoner. The carpet on the broad stairs of the hotel was good enough for me. We climbed to what had been a large double-bedroom on the third floor. A corporal took our names and told us without any sign of interest that the Interrogator would soon arrive.

It was nine o'clock and outside I could see the rain had begun to fall heavily in Marylebone Road, the mist obscuring distant barrage balloons. There was a clock in the waiting-room which ticked annoyingly. I was reminded of the minutes which passed in the dentist's wooden hut as I waited to escape from the camp at Thorn.

Those had been stirring days which I might never experience again. And now, here was London concerned with its own woes, moving slowly and with the maximum of Red Tape. I was sorry for the taxi-driver and his "keb" blown across the road. I wondered what people had endured in the raids and what they had been like. Was it better to have been a prisoner with all the discomfort and frustration of the camp? At least there had been time for reading and reflection and a new understanding of life.

The Man from the War Office was less punctual than the Gestapo and when he did arrive he was an amiable person who asked me very little. The flabby informality of his methods was astonishing.

He handed me a form with a list of questions which I filled in mechanically. The details of my escape seemed to bore him. He only wanted a "rough outline." He introduced me to a younger officer who adopted a different attitude. He took a journalist's interest in my adventures which he eagerly recorded in his interrogation report.

When the interrogation was over we went into a bar at the Transit Camp. Newman, Woollatt and I sat together at a table feeling puzzled by these new surroundings.

A small officer in the uniform of the Coldstream Guards with one arm missing came into the bar. At once I recognised Lt.-Col. Jimmy Langley, M.B.E., M.C., whom I had last seen in hospital at Lille in 1940. From this hospital he had escaped and returned over the Pyrenees.

He asked many questions and spoke knowingly of Maurice and the Greeks. He had information about that mysterious world of underground escape organisations of which as a mere "parcel" I knew very little. Later I was to be closely concerned with their work.

The Commanding Officer of the Transit Camp released us in time for lunch. Hugh Woollatt and I took another taxi and ordered the driver to go to the Berkeley Hotel. We were gay and our conversation was absurd. For me the memory of that taxi drive has poignance, for my companion was killed two years afterwards. All through our journey from the Swiss frontier he had thought only of joining the fight again. That is the main purpose of escaping.

The cloakroom attendant at the Berkeley gingerly placed my curious little bundle of effects well out of reach. I indulged in the exotic luxury of washing my hands among the rich and having my coat brushed. My white shirt was no longer clean and the collar was frayed. I looked at my face in the glass, mischievous and schoolboyish and saw, without embarrassment, the disapproving glance of the attendant.

Smart women were accompanied by officers celebrating their leave. It seemed to us that the women gave us those indulgent glances reserved for schoolboys up for their half-term. Their feathered hats waved imperiously in our direction. Was this England? Could women still buy such hats and indulge in futile gossip?

Years afterwards I watched Schuschnigg, the former Chancellor of Austria, frail and wan after much brutal treatment from the Nazis, dining in the Grand Hotel at Nuremberg. Did the austere Schuschnigg feel, as I had felt in the Berkeley Buttery, that the delights of liberty were only a pleasant illusion dreamed on a two-tiered wooden bed? I remember how his American host led Schuschnigg to a table in the Marble Room at the Grand Hotel where a deafening dance band was playing. Did Schuschnigg feel free? Was this a loosening of the bonds or had he changed one prison for another? I thought of Hermann Goering, a man who had enjoyed luxury and power, lying in his darkened cell in the prison at Nuremberg as the band played in the Marble Room nearby. What did he dream of in those last days of his life?

In the Buttery, I raised my glass and drank to Maurice and his friends. The smart women began to leave the restaurant eyeing us curiously. I was thinking now of my home in Essex and what I should find there in the evening. My mother, desperately ill during the months of my imprisonment, and now recovered a little. The chestnuts in full leaf, the May blossom and the white gates at the beginning of the drive of which I had so vividly dreamed in my cell in the prison of Plock, hourly expecting death. Would it all be real?

Newman and I took the train from Liverpool Street to our homes at Ingatestone. We spoke little, hardly noticing the extraordinary coincidence of our arrival home together. Our approach to the end of the journey was filled with tension and sadness for Newman's father had died only a week before. The train stopped at each station jerking and puffing as of old. Harold Wood, then Brentwood, then Shenfield. From the grimy window, I noticed the familiar signs of my childhood. We two, at the close of our great adventure were unable to grasp that we were home. The emotion of the moment was so strong that I saw the level-crossing gates, the old-fashioned lamps and the chimney pots of the station only as faint images.

My father was alone on the platform. I walked up to him and we said nothing for a moment. It was not a time for words. No sentence which I could have selected would have seemed appropriate. I shook hands with the stationmaster, and then I was in the car travelling along the High Street of Ingatestone, through the hedgerows until we came to the white gates. It was a year and a month since I had lain in the cell at Plock. A year and a month for a vision to become a reality.

In the warm twilight of that May evening I listened to the chimes of Big Ben. They called me back to the wireless hidden under the boards of the camp at Thorn. At nine each night the prisoners in my room would gather close to it, listening to the news through the folds of an overcoat which deadened the sound. Then a courier went along the passages to other rooms reading the news to the prisoners as they lay upon their beds. When I went to bed that night, I looked out over the meadows bathed in moonlight. There was not a sentry box in sight, no wire, no glint of steel. And yet they were with me always, and each night when I heard the chimes of Big Ben I wondered what was happening in the camp.

*   *   *

Slowly I recovered my spirits and lost my sense of persecution. The money accumulated in my bank was large enough to pay for long-awaited comforts. I sauntered down St. James's Street, with twenty pounds to spend, looking into the shop windows. I began with tobacco and cigars, imagining myself a man of leisure, and then ordered two shirts. It was as if I had won a million pounds in a lottery and come home from some lonely island to spend it.

In June 1942 I began to work with Colonel Jimmy Langley and for two years we tried, despite tremendous obstacles, to help the men and women of the Resistance.

There were many enthusiasts for our work, men who had themselves known what it was to be imprisoned. Working with us was Lieutenant-Colonel Ian Garrow, D.S.O., who at the time of my stay in Marseilles had been imprisoned by the French for the part he played in forming the escape organisation. With the help of faithful friends he escaped from prison and came back over the Pyrenees. Pat Windham Wright, M.C. and Bar, who lost an arm in Libya crossed the Channel several times in M.T.B.s to Brittany, before the Normandy invasion, and organised the evacuation of over 100 pilots from the beaches to which they had been escorted by the Resistance.

The underground escape routes expanded all over Europe. Pilots and soldiers came over the Pyrenees bringing tales of heroism. I was often inspired in my work by the memory of the sunset over the Old Port at Marseilles. Who was now sitting in the window seat of Maurice's flat looking out over the shipping?

One day the Gestapo came for Maurice and took him away. Pat, for this was the name of his redoubtable chief, was also a victim of treachery. They took them first to a prison in Paris and then to a concentration camp somewhere in Germany. Yet they survived the brutality of the Gestapo, and Pat went to Buckingham Palace for a George Cross and a D.S.O.

The Greeks and René and Claire escaped over the Pyrenees. I met them when they arrived at Euston, these strangely assorted heroes. They were as urbane but fanatical as they had been in the flat in the Old Port. As Pat's organisation broke up, slowly destroyed by the Gestapo, new heroes and heroines emerged, ready to risk their lives to keep open the escape routes over the mountains. The Belgians particularly distinguished themselves with routes from Brussels to Biarritz and Bilbao.

I learned in the course of these duties so much of unsparing courage and selflessness that the heartless chatter of a cocktail party became difficult to endure. And yet it was at one of these parties that began the healing of my soul. It was a July evening and I was standing in a corner talking to a red-haired girl, and laughed with her at simple things. I found in her the confidence I needed. The veil of depression was lifted—for the first time since I was a prisoner I was gay again. We were soon in love and in a few weeks we were engaged. We were married on a dull December day in Staffordshire by the Bishop of Lichfield, Dr. Edward Woods. It was just a year since I had escaped from Colditz. The Bishop, addressing us, pointed to my rescue from the powers of darkness by the hand of God. And, as he gave his blessing, the sun came suddenly out of the clouds. Its rays shone on the spot where we were standing in the chancel.

There was one more landmark in my journey back to life. I went to Buckingham Palace and stood nervously before a Royal figure in Naval uniform. Far away a string orchestra played in the Throne Room. The King shook me firmly and quietly by the hand and in these simple words restored my faith.

"We are very glad to see you back."

* * *

It was not long before I was in France again. I stepped on to the sandy beach at Courseulles in July, 1944, amid the majestic paraphernalia of the Normandy invasion. My task, under Colonel Jimmy Langley, the little man with one arm whom I had met on the morning of my return to England, was to organise the rescue of servicemen hidden in the forests of Central France and Belgium. There was no more welcome mission, for I remembered the risks that ordinary men and women took in hiding these "evaders." I remembered the strained white faces in the lamplight of the kitchen, the knock at the door and the quick fear in the eyes of simple people.

It was hot and dusty in the lanes of Normandy, churned by tanks and jammed with lorries and the sun beat down upon British armour as it rumbled towards the bocage. Our headquarters were at Creuilly in the cool seclusion of an abbey. At night I lay in a stone bedroom in the abbey tower listening to the frogs croaking unconcernedly among the reeds. And at dawn there came the eternal thunder of artillery in the south. The break-through had begun. I packed my jeep and followed in the wake of the American advance to Avranches. Dead mules, swollen and shrouded in fine dust, barred the roads. In the fields lay cattle and horses killed by shells, and for miles along the road was the odour of antiseptic from a shattered ambulance train. The mules were lifted gingerly aside and the chase gathered momentum to Rennes and Brest. I turned about towards Paris where Patton's Third Army was moving.

The main objective of the rescue operations under Jimmy Langley was to recover a party of Allied pilots and a few soldiers said to be hidden in the forest of Fretteval near Chateaudun. This was achieved after the capture of Le Mans with the help of a Squadron of the Special Air Service under Captain Anthony Greville-Bell, D.S.O. Undiscovered by the Germans, a party of 138 Allied pilots had hidden in the forest for several months, sheltered by rough tents and provisioned by the Maquis. Captain Peter Baker, M.C. (now M.P. for South Norfolk) was sent over the front line with a small advance party and made contact with the men in their woodland "camp."

We went through the enemy lines to get them on a perfect August morning. The jeeps, commandeered Citroëns, and motor-cycles of our weird cavalcade were decked with flowers and at each village girls ran out to us with cakes and wine. The flags of Free France appeared at every window. A few tattered Germans surrendered without resistance. The remainder were straggling back towards the Seine. We loaded the Germans on to our vehicles where they sat looking sadly at the countryside.

Cautiously we approached the forest. There was a loud yell of delight and tattered figures ran from trees and jumped on to our transport. Their faces were weather-beaten and alert as they set up a long cheer at our arrival. Then, as men do, they began to complain of delay. I was mortified to find that two stray American tanks had already arrived upon the scene and had wirelessed for lorries. There were in all one hundred and thirty-eight pilots of different nations and a handful of soldiers. They climbed into buses requisitioned by the Maquis and wildly sang their way back to Le Mans. I greatly enjoyed the gaiety and individualism of this private warfare.

The liberation of Paris was like a fever which, as it waned, left me cold and disconsolate so that I wished to be free of the crowds and on the road to Germany. After a few days the delirium was forgotten in the race for Arnhem. The rapid pursuit of the Germans carried me to Brussels, Eindhoven and then Nijmegen. The road to Nijmegen in the second week of September, 1944, was for many days a tenuous line of attack flanked by the enemy on either side. The transport moving at a snail pace was a perfect target for the bombers which, however, never came.

One rainy evening I reached Nijmegen to learn that the airborne attack of Arnham had failed. Of the First Airborne Division a bare two thousand had been brought over the Rhine to safety. To the forests near Arnhem there fled, so it was said, several hundred officers and men who had evaded capture by the enemy. Many of these, wounded and exhausted, were hidden by Dutch people in their houses. Dutch agents swam across the Rhine to report them in the neighbourhood of Ede some six miles west of Arnhem. Beyond this scanty information little was known of their fate. The grey-faced men in red berets who had escaped capture and staggered out of the storm boats at the end of the battle could tell us little.

I tried to establish an escape route over the Waal from Tiel but Peter Baker who crossed the river in a small boat was taken prisoner by the Germans and the family who sheltered him were shot.

Despite such atrocities the spirit of Resistance in Occupied Holland was fired by the gallant failure of Arnhem. The sacrifice of the First Airborne Division aroused in the Dutch their greatest qualities. From the German frontier to The Hague the starving people rose in revolt, ready to aid the Allies by every means. A week after the battle the number of paratroopers hidden behind the enemy lines and their names and condition became known by a curious circumstance.

The power stations in Nijmegen on the Waal and at Ede on the northern bank of the Rhine were linked by private telephone lines which remained intact while the battle raged. The exchanges were controlled by the Resistance and they gave us the information that in the houses and forests of Ede were hidden nearly one hundred and forty men, among them Major Digby Tatham-Warter, D.S.O.

This officer, a man of calm and ingenuity, conducted the conversations that followed between the two power stations. Despite the risk of capture he came from his hiding place each evening between nine and ten to the terminal house at Ede and there spoke to the rescue organisations in Nijmegen. He passed to those on duty in the power station lists of names of the survivors of the great airborne landing, which included Brigadier Lathbury commanding the First Parachute Brigade.

During the first two weeks of October, 1944, I sat every evening in the gaunt power station with Major Hugh Fraser, M.B.E., of the S.A.S. (now M.P. for Stafford) listening for the telephone bell. It seemed that we were waiting for a signal from the other world. The shells from enemy batteries at Arnhem crashed around the Nijmegen Bridge, shaking the power house. Beside us sat technical officials, their staunch Dutch faces betraying no emotion. We would wait with beating hearts for a faint ring on the telephone and Tatham-Warter's voice.

By this means the rescue of the paratroops over the Rhine was planned. It came to be known as Operation Pegasus. The Dutch Resistance offered to escort the men to the enemy bank if we could organise their evacuation by boat across the river. The place chosen for the crossing was in that dismal low-lying area between the Waal and the Rhine, known to all troops in the fighting in Holland as "The Island." Part of it was held in October, 1944, by the 101st

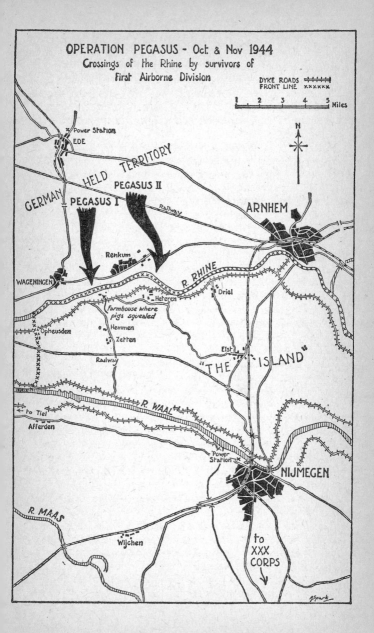

OPERATION PEGASUS – Oct. & Nov. 1944
Crossings of the Rhine by survivors of
First Airborne Division

DYKE ROADS ┼┼┼┼┼┼
FRONT LINE ×××××

1 2 3 4 5 Miles

N

Power Station
EDE

GERMAN HELD TERRITORY

PEGASUS II

PEGASUS I

ARNHEM

Railway

Renkum

R. RHINE

WAGENINGEN

Heteren

Driel

farmhouse where
pigs squealed

Hemmen

Opheusden

Zetten

Elst

"THE" "ISLAND"

Railway

R. WAAL

to Tiel

Afferden

Power
Station

NIJMEGEN

R. MAAS

Wijchen

to
XXX
CORPS

American Airborne Division commanded by Major-General Maxwell Taylor. There was little activity on either bank, the enemy holding their line with a few Companies of Infantry. Some days before Pegasus there appeared on the scene after a lone escape over the river Lieutenant-Colonel David Dobie, D.S.O., of the 1st Parachute Battalion who brought news of the survivors and took command of the scheme of rescue.

As the sun began to set on the evening of the 20th October, 1944, there was silence on the river front. With Hugh Fraser, I crept through a village sheltering beneath the dyke which held back the river. We made our way silently, following the white tapes laid out by American paratroops, to a farm-house in the fields below the level of the dyke, and sat on iron bedsteads as guns and mortars opened up on either bank.

Shortly before midnight we left the farm-house and moved towards the bank, following the white tape, and watched dim shapes of men carrying assault boats. Their boots squelched in the muddy fields. Then, from the rear, came the sharp crack of a Bofors gun sending a stream of tracer-shells across the river. The gun, fired at an angle of 45 degrees, was a homing signal to the escape party approaching the enemy bank. Every fifteen minutes after midnight it fired its twelve rounds to guide the parachuters home.

Suddenly there was a squeal of little pigs. Someone had trodden on a litter. The squealing which followed lasted several minutes. It was an anxious moment for sounds carried far across the river and the enemy would be ready with their Spandau machine-guns on the other side.

I began to cough and had to stuff a handkerchief in my mouth. The American Commander and Hugh Fraser moved forward to the side of another farm-house and I stumbled after them. I could now see the dark shape of the river and hear the faint ripple of water beneath the bank. I strained my eyes for flashes in Morse from a torch opposite, the signal arranged with Tatham-Warter on the telephone.

Half an hour passed. I thought of the Rhine flowing eternally towards the sea careless of the fears and anxieties of soldiers. The Vistula, huge and brown, and filled with refuse, had cared no more about Forbes and I as we sat on the shingle and cooled our blistered feet in 1941. The escape in Poland seemed a century ago.

The pigs had now gone to sleep and a slight breeze blew from the enemy bank. The Bofors fired its signal above us and the tracer-shells were reflected in the dark water. From the enemy side the rosy light of six-barrelled mortars— "Moaning Minnies," also illuminated the river as they fired into the American lines. The glow over the water reminded me of the procession of boats in the light of fireworks, on the fourth of June at Eton in the piping days of peace.

Each man was peering silently across the river waiting for the torchlight. Then it appeared so close that the escaping party seemed within a few yards of us over the dark water. A whispered order and the American paratroops and Royal Engineers carrying the assault boats to the bank launched them with astonishing speed. The splash of oars and the scraping noise of rowlocks around us were uncomfortably loud. Then came a short uncertain burst of rifle fire at the very crossing place. We listened tensely but no cries came from the other side. Twenty minutes passed and then in terrible excitement we heard the assault boats returning smoothly over the water. They touched down one by one against the mud bank. Figures of men appeared before me feeling their way and following the white tape across the farmland to safety. First came the tall figure of Brigadier Lathbury, bare-headed in civilian clothes. The airborne officers and men, 140 in number, moved across the fields to another farmhouse where the Americans with unexampled organisation had prepared hot coffee and doughnuts.

At the end of October 1944, plans were made for a further rescue attempt called Pegasus Two. The point chosen for the crossing of the escapers was further up the Rhine at Heteren near Wageningen. At Wageningen a few months later, Allied Staff officers had their first armistice discussions with Seyss-Inquart, the Protector of Holland. Artur Seyss-Inquart, a lame Austrian lawyer, was second-in-command to Hans Frank in Poland, and later the persecutor of the Dutch. A year after, as I entered his cell in Nuremberg prison, he received me with thin-lipped politeness, refusing ever to unbend or acknowledge the least blame for his cruelties in Poland and Holland.

Pegasus Two failed with serious casualties. On the night of the operation there came a high wind which drowned every sound upon the river and lashed the water into small waves. Our joint headquarters with the American paratroops was in the cellar of a house on the dyke. We watched throughout the night for a torch signal from the other side. The Bofors went on firing tracer-shells across the river but no one came to the far bank. I decided to watch again the next evening and returned to hear from American paratroops that a man with an Irish accent had been shouting to them across the river. At dark, a storm boat crossed and returned with two strange characters in civilian clothes. One was an Irishman called O'Casey and the other a Dutchman. After they had drunk liberally from a jar of rum they were able to tell us that the column of escapers on the way to the bank had been intercepted by the Germans and dispersed. Most of the men who sought safety in the woods were finally captured or killed.

At midnight, another voice was heard calling across the river and a strapping American lieutenant volunteered to go across in a canoe. The current was swift and treacherous but he reached the far bank and by walkie-talkie told us that he had found a paratrooper and would bring him back. We waited for them but there was no sound save the lapping of the river against the dyke. After half an hour came reports of despairing cries for help down stream. Neither of the men were ever seen again and there was no report of their bodies being washed ashore within our lines.

It was dawn when I crawled sadly from the farm-house cellar at Heteren. The rain had begun to fall, swamping the fields, so that the flowers planted on a soldier's grave were washed away. The wind blew among the broken wires hanging from the few remaining telegraph poles along the road. My jeep slithered through the mud of farm tracks and back again to the roadway until through the blinding rain I could see the outline of the Nijmegen Bridge. Two shells whined over the bridge bursting among the rubble of the town. The column of transport in front of me moved slowly forward among the network of iron and raced up the far bank to escape the murderous shelling from the heights of Arnhem.

I watched the Waal, dark and angrily swollen with rain,

flowing beneath the bridge and bending out of sight beyond the power station. I was thinking of a summer's day in 1940 when the barge carrying prisoners of war to Germany struggled upstream beneath the bridge. The men were crowded in the sooty holds or clustered on the hatches watching the old houses and towers of the ancient city. I was hungry and forlorn, fingering a piece of mildewed bread and wondering whether to throw it into the stream or in my desperation to eat it and risk the consequences. There was a chorus of whistling and laughter from the prisoners. Girls in summer dresses were bicycling across the bridge waving to the barge below. And now it seemed that this gaunt bridge must always be associated in my mind with misery or fear. Another shell, with a noise like an approaching train, flew past the bridge and burst not far ahead among the lorries and jeeps. I passed the blood and wreckage on my way to the headquarters of XXX Corps to report the disaster of Pegasus Two.

CHAPTER XIV

In August, 1940 when the barge filled with prisoners had passed beneath the Nijmegen bridge it continued slowly towards the junction of the Rhine and the Waal. From the crowded deck, I had seen the confluence of the great rivers and a few miles up the Rhine the barge reached the inland port of Emmerich at dawn and was moored at the quayside. The prisoners climbed down rope ladders clutching their miserable bundles. They waited on the quayside while German under-officers strutted past their ranks staring at them contemptuously. The prisoners, realising that they were at last on German soil, were silent.

Five years afterwards when the war in Holland was over I drove to Emmerich again through scarred fields and broken trees. The goods yard near the station was hardly discernible in the chaos. Beside it in 1940 there had been a kind of recreation ground, an open field for games such as you might see in any English town. It was in this field in August, 1940, that the occupants of the barges had been herded to wait for the train to take them further inland to captivity. It was here that I sat on the hard turf eating a ration of mildewed bread. In that corner where the bomb craters now overlapped each other in a confusion of broken tiles and bricks and earth, I had talked with three German soldiers. They were middle-aged and corpulent and their voices were loud, unfriendly and irritating.

"England," said a huge man with two gold teeth in a coarse hatchet face, "will never win. She must surrender now."

I looked at the dogged British prisoners resting on the ground. They understood no German.

"Do you hear what these Jerries are telling me?" I said, repeating the German words in English.

There was a good-natured but feeble jeering. The mildewed bread had had its effect and many were faint in the hot sun. Colonel Kennedy of the 4th Oxford and Bucks Light infantry, his arm in a sling, but still military and correct, turned to me.

"You tell them that England will never surrender," he said gruffly.

"England will never surrender," I shouted back in German.

The guards stopped talking, remained silent for some moments, then laughed in a harsh guttural way. The prisoners looked up from the grass in tired surprise. The guards began to sulk and complained that the prisoners were too well treated. They took their rifles from their shoulders and began to make animal noises. They jabbed the barrels of their rifles towards the men on the ground. A German under-officer hearing their shouts came over to investigate.

"In war," he said portentously, "there are no politics."

In August, 1945, this scene was vividly in my mind as I stood among the bomb craters, my boots covered with thick dust. I followed the same route which I had taken as a prisoner towards the cattle trucks waiting in the goods yard. It was difficult to find the way. The craters extended over the roadway to the smashed yard. The siding from which the trucks, filled to the brim with sweating prisoners, had left five years before was impossible to distinguish. The rails rose into the air with their sleepers twisted into gaunt surrealist shapes. I stood looking down the line towards Germany. This way the prisoners had gone to Iserlohn in the stifling heat of 1940.

I walked back to my jeep and then drove towards the Ruhr, navigating great clusters of bricks and glass and craters. At evening I reached Iserlohn, headquarters of British First Corps. I stopped at the station where the prisoners, staggering from the closed cattle trucks, had been blinded by the light before being lined up and marched to Hemer. Here a great gaunt unfinished barracks had been set aside for them. Now with a queer sense of homecoming I walked again through the gates, where German civilians had stared in silence, into the barrack rooms, searching among the cheerless passages for a room on the first floor. It was not difficult to find. Here I had lain ill on a pile of straw, beside the other wounded who had come there with me from France.

In this room I first thought of escape. I had begun in this unfriendly place to think of imprisonment as a new phase of living, not, as some did, as the end of life. I used to sit in the straw talking of the future to John Surtees, M.C. of the Rifle Brigade. He was very young with blond hair and he was an officer of great determination. Months afterwards he jumped from the train on the way to Thorn and was free for several days until a farmer found him sleeping in a barn. He deserved more success. He had the escaper's temperament and the courage to jump from a train moving through a hostile land at night. It seemed to some of us in 1940 that imprisonment was a spur to new achievement. Material rewards were not the final objectives of the escaper, however much he might dream of soft beds and pints of beer. His real purpose was to overcome by every means the towering obstacles in his way.

At the end of August, 1945, I was appointed to the British War Crimes Executive at Bad Oeynhausen, the head-quarters of 21 Army Group. British War Crimes Executive was an organisation set up to collect evidence against the principal Nazi war criminals. Members of its staff led by the Attorney-General, Sir Hartley Shawcross, Q.C., subsequently conducted the case for the prosecution at Nuremberg. My qualifications for joining it were a moderate knowledge of German and what seemed, after these adventurous years, a very distant connection with the law.

Many of the officers who helped to collect evidence against Goering and his fellow-prisoners spoke German fluently.

Some had been prisoners of war for several years. One of them, Major Wolfe Frank, himself a German from Munich was in the British Army and became the best interpreter at the trial.

I did not join this organisation with any revengeful spirit. I had my triumph over the Germans on the day when Luteyn and I crossed into Switzerland. The cowbells we heard over snow-covered fields and the circus poster that showed us that we had got through were memories transcending any bitterness. For me freedom was a greater prize than vengeance. Yet the first mission I received from the British War Crimes Executive awakened many old fears. I was sent to Essen to collect evidence against Gustav Krupp von Bohlen und Halbach, head of the great armament firm.

How futile it now seems!

When I drove to Essen, the jeep, driven by a Tyneside corporal, jolted its way through the great destruction. Huge chimneys stood gaunt and black against the sunset. But Essen was not dead. A heart beat faintly under the tangled mass of steel and stone. As I passed the vast Krupp factory I saw the sunset reflected in its broken windows as if furnaces still burned within.

Beyond the city we drove into the hills among the neat houses and came at nightfall to the former home of an industrial magnate called the Villa Tengelmann. The house, used as an officers' mess for North German Coal Control, was filled with Hogarth prints and fake antiques.

Every morning I drove from the Villa Tengelmann to the Villa Huegel, the Krupp palace high above. A long drive, overgrown with cedars, wound towards the house where visitors in carriages and cars had driven to pay their respects to the dynasty of Krupp. Even the vulgar Nazis were sometimes asked to dinner. I thought of them being received by a butler at the door. The mansion rose before me like a vast old-fashioned battleship. Its ugliness took my breath away. Ostentatious and forbidding, it frowned sourly on the visitor.

The Krupp butler was no longer there. He lived in a cottage nearby, surveying the British officials from time to time with frozen hostility as he gave them his advice and information about their fantastic headquarters. He had been there, so it was said, when the mansion was captured and when paratroops appeared at the front door armed with grenades he told them with great dignity:

"Mr. Krupp will be most upset about this."

"Mr. Krupp" was Alfried Krupp, the eldest son of the family who succeeded his father in the management of the great works towards the end of the war. His father, the man I came to prosecute, Gustav Krupp von Bohlen und Halbach, was not a Krupp at all. He married "Big Bertha" Krupp, grand-daughter of the founder of the firm and by her had several sons and daughters. Their colossal portraits hung in an entrance hall larger than that of the Waldorf Astoria in New York.

It was a monstrous place, this palace of an industrial empire. Portraits nine feet high, portrayed three generations of proud Krupps on sofas or standing majestically beside their gilded furniture. Both furniture and portraits were crude in their hugeness. They were pitiful in their attempt to increase the stature of the Krupps. The chairs and tables of abnormal height contributed to the distortion of size. Here were people who had tried to conceal their smallness with great baubles.

I was accompanied to Essen by Major Peter Casson of the British War Crimes Executive. He was a big humorous man and together we found much to laugh at as we searched the mansion. In several of the enormous rooms the Coal Control had their offices and here we rummaged in safes and drawers hunting for evidence to support the alleged conspiracy of Gustav Krupp von Bohlen with Hitler to wage war against the civilised world.

Gustav emerged from the pile of family photographs as a slight, silver-haired and prim business man. From uncertain reports he was now living in a hunting-lodge near Salzburg with Bertha. He seemed to bear little resemblance to the stern well-posed portraits of the family of Friedrich Krupp.

I sat among the filing cabinets studying the photographs. Krupp von Bohlen in his study; Krupp von Bohlen with the Duke of Windsor visiting the works; Krupp von Bohlen out shooting, and Krupp von Bohlen at the wedding of one of his family to a Nazi. In these photographs the tall figures of Bertha and Alfried Krupp seemed to dwarf Gustav Krupp von Bohlen. It was a fascinating study from which I derived many hours of enjoyment.

The Krupp archives were in an underground room beneath the mansion with filing cabinets at each corner. Many private papers had already been moved by the family. There remained carbon copies of quantities of private letters from Krupp von Bohlen typed on expensive notepaper. The letters revealed an irritating self-importance. It seemed to me that the Krupps had little taste or discrimination but much arrogance. Their photographs showed clearly the power and influence which they enjoyed among the Nazis. Soon their social tyrannies ceased to absorb my interest. I was concerned in those September days with finding evidence of their guilt. It was not difficult to connect Gustav Krupp von Bohlen with the allegations in the indictment but of his guilt or innocence the world has heard little for he was never tried. Alfried Krupp has served the sentence imposed on him at a later trial and has now been released to become the richest man in the world.

It was a hot August and the dust of Essen was in my throat. The stench of death was in the streets and I had a feeling of being in the presence of a wounded animal. Peter Casson and I drove through crowds of working people to the Krupp factory. Only the main office building was largely intact. The remainder, foundries and machine shops, were damaged and inert. In the offices, however, there was life and the planning of new projects. Here was the core, the heart of the monster. I watched the directors, managers and secretaries working busily.

Back at the Villa Huegel in the evening we talked of cold steel forged in secret. It could be done again. Had not Krupp von Bohlen boasted of his defiance of the Treaty of Versailles?

The telephone rang from First Corps Headquarters. A voice ordered me to arrest most of the directors and managers for interrogation and to search the entire works the following morning. This was a fabulous order. I went into the library of the mansion used as an officers' mess and sat down to think in a fat, maroon leather chair. It seemed the most extraordinary order I had received over five adventurous years, and yet the most stimulating.

At eight o'clock armoured cars of the Manchester Regiment bounded over the bomb-torn roads to the centre of Essen. Peter Casson and I followed with a row of jeeps filled with Field Security Police. Field Security Police! I laughed to myself for I had had experience of the Security Police of Heinrich Himmler. "S.D." men they were called. Big thug-like Germans in civilian clothes indistinguishable from the Gestapo. Their methods differed widely from the compara-tively courteous denazification system of the British F.S.P., many of them scholarly sergeants in spectacles. I laughed again when I thought of the great procession of German Field Police and guards assembled to search for Forbes and myself as we stood inside the wire of the camp at Thorn.

It was my turn to wield the big stick, to shout like a con-queror, but I was not jack-booted and I had only a handful of cheerful Englishmen to help me master the whole Krupp Empire. The armoured cars surrounded the battered works. They seemed puny and ineffective beside the great chim-neys. The soldiers and policemen ran to guard each door locking the office staff inside. Angry Teutonic faces stared from the windows. The women secretaries, hard-faced and scowling, stood to attention at the desks as investigators began to search drawers and filing cabinets. It was a hope-less task. Incriminating documents had been burned long ago. There were a few documents relating to the employ-ment of foreign workers by Krupps which seemed to in-criminate both Gustav and Alfried.

I turned my attention to the directors. Some were classi-fied as Nazis. They lived in the relics of expensive houses in different parts of Essen. Their tumbledown dwellings were filled with uninvited lodgers. They went meekly enough to the prison of Essen, where a few cells were undamaged, guarded by Field Security Police and Germans. In a cellar Casson and I conducted interrogations probing into the res-ponsibility of Krupps for the ill-treatment of foreign workers alleged in the indictment. The allegations were serious. It was said that many foreign nationals had suf-fered and died at the hands of the firm. I inspected a nar-row iron box sufficient only in size for a man to survive in a painfully cramped position. It was said that recalcitrant workers had been locked in this box by the Krupp foremen. Whatever the directors knew about such treatment they would give nothing away. They refused to betray Gustav and Alfried and two of them attempted suicide rather than admit the truth.

Whilst the interrogation of the Krupp directors was continuing in the prison our small British War Crimes team was joined by a number of Americans. They were led by a tall Jewish lawyer, Captain Sam Harris, a person of the greatest industry and perseverance. Together we set up an office on the outskirts of Essen to sift the Krupp diaries and correspondence for evidence to support the indictment. The American team was composed of G.I.s of some scholastic distinction, many of them of German birth and all of Jewish origin. The speed with which they set about the investigation of everything that was even faintly prejudicial, anything which had the slightest odour of collaboration with Hitler, filled me with mixed admiration and alarm. Together we searched every nook and cranny of the Villa Huegel, sounding the walls for secret safes. Two of the safes we discovered, in the bedroom and dressing-room of Gustav and Bertha Krupp, defied attempts to open them for many days.

The excitement attending their eventual opening was one of the strangest episodes of my stay in Essen. The safe in Gustav's dressing-room was embedded in concrete in the wall of the house. For a long time it remained entirely concealed from our investigation team. Its existence was revealed by a former private secretary who after close questioning agreed to point out where it lay. An elderly German of forbidding appearance, she advanced into the dressing-room. She stood pointing dramatically at the corner of the room and exclaiming:

"There!"

Slowly the oak panelling in the wall swung back, revealing the bronze doors of the safe. The keys produced were useless for someone had tampered with the locks. I sent immediately for the Royal Engineers who with much parapernalia arrived upon the scene and began to burn through the bronze on the outer part of the door. Next came a heavy layer of brass and then, to my consternation, a thickness of steel plate. I could not believe that further protective armour was to follow. But after the steel there was a thickness of copper and then another plate of steel. Then came the final obstacle which postponed work upon the safe for many days, for after the last thickness of steel was a great slab of concrete.

A crowd of people stood in tense expectancy as efforts were made to dislodge the safe from the wall. When this failed the engineers again turned their attention to the lock. It was due to be opened in the presence of so large a company of senior officers and officials, of almost every department of the British Army and Control Commission, that Gustav's dressing-room could scarcely hold them. A sweating sergeant of the Royal Engineers worked on the lock to an accompaniment of Cockney expletives. He dismantled it piece by piece until the moment came to open the door. There was a hush in the panelled room. I fidgeted nervously. Then the door opened with a smart click and there came a ripple of laughter. The safe was nearly empty!

I could find nothing but a few old bills and envelopes. In the safe in Bertha's bedroom were a few empty jewel cases. Peter Casson and I sat on the edge of an enormous bath with gold taps of outsize dimensions and roared with laughter.

The massive safes made in the Krupp works symbolised the might and bombast of the family enterprise. I determined to see these Krupp giants face to face. I knew only that Gustav was at Salzburg and Alfried in a concentration camp at Sachsenhausen. When, therefore, our team had almost completed its exhausting task of studying the firm's documents, Peter Casson and I set off to Nuremberg where the trial of Goering and his colleagues was due to begin, to find further news of Krupp von Bohlen.

It seemed fitting to me that Gustav Krupp von Bohlen, snobbish no doubt about the Nazis, should be tried in the capital of Hitlerism. The overlord of a great arms industry, whose employees had asserted that the major part of their business was the production of agricultural implements and lawnmowers, should defend himself in public.

The Americans who formed the staff of the United States Chief Prosecutor, Justice Jackson, eagerly awaited the results of our investigation. Then came infuriating news, which made all our work at Essen seem wasted. Someone discovered that the overlord was senile and unfit to stand his trial. The days spent in rummaging among his archives and safes had been in vain. After these feverish operations he was to escape justice. How it was that the Allied authorities failed to discover beforehand whether he was fit to take his trial, I have never discovered. When the ruins of

Berlin collapsed, bringing the end of Adolf Hitler and his 1,000 year Reich, Krupp von Bohlen, lord of the Villa Huegel, was hardly alive. In August of 1945 he was no more than a baby unable to speak or feed himself.

Early in October when the International Military Tribunal at Nuremberg instructed me to serve upon Goering and the other Defendants copies of the indictment in which they were named, Mr. James H. Rowe, jr., formerly one of President Roosevelt's personal staff, travelled to the Krupp hunting-lodge with a copy of the indictment. He found an old man under the care of nurses, unable to talk, and left the copy of the indictment on the bed. Krupp von Bohlen's mind was as empty as the safes in the Villa Huegel.

The allied doctors sent by the International Military Tribunal to examine him, reported that he was suffering from senile softening of the brain and that his condition was unlikely to improve. They were of the opinion that he was unfit mentally and physically to appear at Nuremberg. "He was indifferent and apathetic and his face was mask-like. Only painful and disagreeable stimuli produced any reaction and then it was merely a facial expression of discontent sometimes accompanied by grunts of disapproval."

It seemed from information supplied by Bertha Krupp that in 1943 Gustav had had a stroke which impaired the function of the right side of his body and since the beginning of 1945 he had only spoken an occasional single word apart from expletives, such as *Ach Gott*, and *Donner Wetter*, when disturbed.

In October, I was an official of the Nuremberg Tribunal when the judges decided that Gustav should not be tried.

I left the room in the Palace of Justice after the judges and prosecutors had debated his fate and drove in a jeep into the centre of Nuremberg. The ancient walls of the castle were breached and broken and the old houses familiar to Dürer had collapsed in piles of splintered wood. I walked over to the main station of Nuremberg and looked at the broken roof and twisted girders. In the booking-hall and waiting-rooms half-starved Germans huddled for warmth. These sad figures, sleeping in the dusk, were the victims of the Revolution of Destruction. Luteyn and I must have looked much the same three years ago as we changed trains at Regensburg. The American Military Police were directing the huge crowds of dejected travellers as I went back to the Grand Hotel and up the steps through the swing doors and into the bar. There were loud voices from officers of many nations in khaki uniforms. Their American girl friends, secretaries of the staff of the United States prosecution, danced with them to a German band, with a meagre repertoire, which played in the "Marble Room" next door. Suddenly, the room burst into a solid jitter-bugging uproar fit to wake the dead. At that moment I thought that Krupp von Bohlen unable to speak or understand or commune with the outer world had scored a victory over the victors.

CHAPTER XV

OF the many consequences of my escape from Colditz my appointment as an official of the International Military Tribunal was the least expected. I became a kind of liaison officer between the tribunal and the defendants. I felt a sense of subtle irony in my position. Most of the men and women who took part in the struggle against Hitler would have given much to be in my place. Goering, Ribbentrop, Streicher; the names were household words. Among the ruined homes of ordinary people, in concentration camps, and in the ranks of fighting men these names spelled cruelty and bad faith. The representatives of nations might journey to Nuremberg to see them in the dock, but it fell to me, their one-time prisoner, to meet them face to face within the narrow walls of their cells.

On the afternoon of October 18th, 1945 I went with Mr. Harold B. Willey, the General Secretary of the Tribunal, to serve copies of the indictment on the prisoners. Colonel Andrus, U.S. Army, the prison governor, led us along a covered pathway to the main entrance of the prison. My mind was back again among the jangling of keys in the prison of Plock. Two tiers of cells rose on either side like the walls of a dark canyon. The iron gates of the main entrance were closed behind us. It was like entering a dungeon of despair.

We signed a book and walked to the far end of the prison, led by Colonel Andrus and a white-helmeted gaoler with a bunch of keys on a huge ring. Behind us, came a procession of orderlies bearing copies of the bulky indictment and a retinue of prison officials. An interpreter came with me so that there should be no inaccuracies in my advice to the prisoners as to their rights under the Charter of the Tribunal.

Hermann Goering stood beside his bed. It seemed for a moment that his enormous body would topple back on to the American Army blankets. He swayed a little and his long mouth twitched in a curious fashion. He looked like a man discovered without his false teeth. I did not know then that he had good natural teeth. He had been asleep when we entered. The strange way in which his lips moved did not seem of importance. Afterwards, I wondered if it was the clue to a great mystery. Was there a tiny phial of poison wedged between his teeth? Had we surprised him with his secret means of suicide?

He gave me a comic bow as the prison officials gathered round me. After a moment his lips ceased to move and he was no longer, so it seemed, embarrassed by our entrance. With one hand he pointed to his bed.

"I am afraid I cannot offer you a chair," he said politely.

I could not help smiling at his aplomb. It seemed only yesterday that Goering had come to see the preparations on the French coast for the invasion of Britain.

In July, 1940, the wounded from the defence of Calais were being evacuated to Lille in lorries and buses. Along the road from St. Omer a cavalcade of huge Mercedes cars swept past the wounded on their way to Calais.

"That was the Reichsmarschall—unser Hermann!" said an excited German.

So what? I was too weak to care. We were just a party of convalescent officers jolting over the roads in a French bus. From the Rifle Brigade, Captain Peter Peel and John Surtees, from the K.R.R.C., Lieutenants Alan Wigan and Charlie Madden, were my companions. Sometimes we lost touch with the Germans guarding the convoy of wounded and stopped to receive wine and offers of help from the sympathetic French. It would have been easy for me to escape from the convoy for I was the only one of the five officers who had not been hit in the leg. The wounds in my side were healed. I lacked only the physical strength and determination to seize the opportunity. When I next thought of escape I was behind barbed wire.

Here then was the Reichsmarschall, a small fat man in dove grey. He was thinner, nevertheless, than the figure on the screen in the cinema at Leipzig where Luteyn and I had sheltered from the cold in 1942. His soft hands no longer bore splendid jewelled rings as they had done in his days of luxury and political power.

I explained my duties to him with confidence. He seemed so much a part of the history of the last few years that I was surprised at my own self-assurance. He listened, and suddenly his mood changed to one of depression.

"So it has come."

The fruity rasping voice was still there without the bombast and heartiness of the days of his popularity.

I asked him whether he wished for counsel of his own choice, or for the Tribunal to appoint one for him.

"I have nothing whatever to do with lawyers. You will have to find one for me. Personally I do not think that any German lawyer would dare to speak in front of this Allied Tribunal. Would it not be better if I were to defend myself?"

"I think you would be well advised to have someone to appear for you."

"It all seems pretty hopeless to me. I must read this indictment very carefully, but I do not see how it can have any basis in law."

"This is a subject which you had best discuss with a lawyer acting for you."

"Lawyers will be no use in this trial. What is required is a good interpreter. I want my own private interpreter during the trial."

"You had better ask the Tribunal about that. I shall be coming to see you tomorrow about your counsel."

Goering again bowed cumbrously and seemed to be ushering us out of his cell. I turned to watch him and caught, so it seemed, a trace of geniality in his small greedy eyes.

When the door of Goering's cell was closed and the key turned in the lock, I felt a sense of great relief that the ordeal had passed. Yet the drama was for me a strange anti-climax. I had half-expected a legendary monster of cruelty and vice. I found that I had crossed Europe to meet a decayed and gloomy voluptuary.

The atmosphere of decay, almost of dissolution, persisted as we entered the cells of these broken men. I felt no pity, I was too aware of their crimes. I could almost hear the cries of the tortured man in the prison at Plock. I had no emotion but merely surprise that I should find myself so close to them. It seemed almost beyond belief.

"Whose cell do we visit next?" I said to Colonel Andrus.

"Hess," he said, "now we shall see some fun."

The key turned in the lock with a smooth sound that brought a small sharp pang of remembrance.

Rudolf Hess, deputy of the Fuehrer, stood within a yard of me as the door opened. A burly military policeman pushed his way forward and clapped handcuffs round his thin wrists. Hess remained still. His eyes in their dark sockets were level with mine, looking straight through me. His great black brows were lifted in faint wonderment. A schoolboy-ish grin broke over his face as he lifted up his manacled hands in a queer gesture of derision. It was as if he were about to say:

"I am not as mad as they think. I shall not hurt you."

After the trial began he was no longer handcuffed. I saw him on numerous occasions in his cell and in a room at the Palace of Justice and I always found him lucid, sometimes humorous. On this October afternoon he still wore the Luftwaffe flying boots, relics of his strange flight to Scotland in 1941. How long ago it all seemed! I had half-forgotten the little *Hauptmann* in the train to Colditz and his enormous ugly wife. I felt almost an affection for them. They had provided an amusing incident in my journey from one prison to another. I could see the look of puzzled indignation as the woman exclaimed:

"I don't see how he got that aeroplane!"

That was what the world, including Hermann Goering, Reichsmarschall of the Luftwaffe, had said.

The hero of this memorable flight remained motionless as I explained the purpose of my visit. He stared into the middle distance as if he were proudly watching a vast parade at the Party Rally at Nuremberg. He grinned again, baring his white teeth, then suddenly began to writhe and groan.

"Stomach cramps, I guess," said Colonel Andrus.

Evidently the pain subsided swiftly. I handed him the indictment. Hess took the document and said:

"Can I defend myself?"

"Yes, by Article 16 of the Charter of the Tribunal."

"Then I wish to do so."

"I would not advise you to do so. It is in your own interest to have a lawyer."

This was the moment which I had feared, for the Allied Judges were nervous that if Hess was permitted to defend himself he would turn the Tribunal proceedings into a pantomime. I did not, however, think fit to press the matter that afternoon for there were other visits to be made and the keys were jangling impatiently. I turned to go, but Hess said quietly:

"May I ask another question?"

I nodded.

"Am I to be tried with Goering and the other Party comrades who are in the cells here?"

"You are charged with taking part in a conspiracy with Goering and other members of the National Socialist Party, therefore you will all be tried together upon these charges."

I felt a little pompous, like a young police officer cautioning his first offender. Hess winced and looked at me with an expression of disdain in his mad eyes. He turned his emaciated body towards the bed.

"I do not like to be tried with Goering," he said primly.

We walked out of the cell and the door was shut. I looked through the inspection window in the door. Hess was seated on his bed with the bulky indictment beside him, reading an English novel with a coloured dust-jacket.

High in the roof of the prison sounded the shouts of guards and the familiar noise of containers dragged over metal flooring. I began to feel tired and oppressed by the prison. The American policemen, apparently unmoved, led me to another cell. I could see the face of the occupant through the window. A trim little man was looking at me with blue eyes and a large strawberry-coloured nose. He had a bald forehead suggesting intellectual strength. The door opened with a flourish and showed him standing as his fellow-member of the General Staff, Wilhelm Keitel had been, in an old tunic with grey breeches. Instead of black boots he also wore felt slippers. Quietly, he stood to attention like a respectful groom waiting to receive instructions for his master's carriage. There was an impatient pause as Colonel Andrus and the other officials took up their positions around me and I began to speak.

"Alfried Jodl?"

"Yes."

Colonel-General Jodl, Chief of Staff of the High Command of the German Armed Forces was looking critically at my Sam Browne. He displayed no emotion, and when I explained my mission to him, he began to speak with brisk efficiency. I could imagine him at staff conferences, lucid, courteous but relentless.

"Will you advise me, Herr Major, what sort of lawyer I should have to defend me?"

"What do you mean?"

I was a little nonplussed. Jodl continued incisively as if he were addressing some ill-informed official.

"I wish to know whether it would be best to have as my advocate a lawyer who is an expert in international law, or one who is expert in criminal law?"

"The indictment charges you with crimes against international law. I can ascertain for you the qualifications of the persons on this list of lawyers. I should think you need an expert in both branches."

Little Jodl was a staff officer close to Hitler, but he was not the criminal type. He was placid as he stood there before me. His hands were steady as he fingered the indictment.

"I shall read this document and consider the point. I am already preparing my defence. You will understand how difficult it is without paper or pencils. Can you help me to get some?"

I understood more than Jodl would ever know. For a moment I felt a half-amused compassion for the efficient General Staff officer deprived of paper! There was no self-pity in him, no tears. Thus he must have looked over the years as he perfected Hitler's military plans to dominate the world by force. In the same calm fashion must he have agreed to the shooting of unarmed prisoners of war. That is why he paid the penalty of hanging, but polite and competent to the last.

I did not enjoy my reception in the cells of Jodl or Grand-Admiral Doenitz, the Commander in Chief of Hitler's fleet.

I could not escape a feeling of embarrassment. These high officers, shorn of their insignia and decorations, still carefully brushed their clothes. Even prisoners of war at Colditz and Spangenburg had been allowed to keep their badges of rank. These men, famous in their own land, wore the garments of humiliation, coarse prison clothes. At their interrogation or in Court they were allowed their uniforms, shorn of any distinction. I could sympathise with those who wore rough prison clothes, painful to the skin.

Grand-Admiral Karl Doenitz roused less sympathy in me than Jodl. Here was the man whom Hitler, in his last ravings in the shelter beneath Berlin Chancellery, appointed as his successor. Hitler's political testament directed Doenitz to "uphold the racial laws in all their severity and mercilessly resist the universal poisoner of all nations, international Jewry."

Doenitz was nervous and apprehensive. His hands fingered the side of his prison trousers. He took the document enquiringly and sighed. There was fear in his eyes and then a rallying of his old faith. He began to speak like a Grand-Admiral.

"What am I to be tried for?"

"Please read the indictment and you will discover. I shall come to see you tomorrow."

Doenitz looked at me warily and handed me a small piece of paper. Written on it were the words "Flottenrichter Otto Kranzbuehler."

This was the name of a Fleet Advocate serving in the still mobilised part of the German Minesweeping Service at Hamburg in the British Zone. It was my duty to obtain such lawyers as the Defendants required and I promised Doenitz that he should be defended if possible by one of his own Naval officers.

Indeed the Royal Navy sent Kranzbuehler without delay and he arrived in Nuremberg within a few days of my first meeting with Doenitz.

Doenitz bowed and, as I turned to go, he looked despairingly at the indictment but did not speak. He was forlorn, no longer the guardian of the Sacred Myth, but I did not trust his fierce blue eyes.

The characters in this remarkable tragedy of History were swiftly revealed to me as talking waxworks. Robert

Ley, leader of the Labour Front, old and decayed by alcohol, slobbered as if he were still under its influence. He looked at me hazily. In the last week in October when I interviewed him in a room in the Palace of Justice about his counsel he began to rave and shout. He said that, in framing the Articles of the Charter of the Tribunal under which he was to be tried, the Allies had made the Ten Commandments which they had broken themselves. As he walked from the room back to his cell he still seemed drunk and unsteady. Within half an hour he had torn up his khaki-coloured American towel into strips, made it into a rope, stuffed his mouth with rags, and hanged himself from the latrine waste-pipe in the wall. When they found him he was dead.

The lords of the New Order succeeded each other, each more wretched than the last. Here was Dr. Walter Funk, once President of the Reichsbank and Minister of Economics. He wore in his cell a long overcoat by special permission of the prison office. His flabby face was the colour of ancient dough and wore a look of abject misery. It was difficult to believe that this dejected person had served in any government. Yet, one of the principal accusations against him was the storing of gold, extracted from the teeth of concentration camp victims, in the vaults of the Reichsbank. He winced when he was addressed, particularly when his name was pronounced phonetically by American guards. He took the indictment and began to weep in a slow and ludicrous fashion. The tears rolled down his heavy face.

After a minute Funk dried his tears and apologised.

"I must see my counsel at once," he pleaded in a doleful voice. "I have a great interest in the outcome of this trial," he said.

"So has the whole world," I replied, "and the Tribunal does not intend that there should be any delay in its opening. I will get your counsel as soon as I can."

I was tempted to say that the trial was of interest to the relatives of those whose gold teeth were deposited in the Reichsbank.

Each cell I visited increased the exhaustion of my mind. It was more than three hours before I had seen all of the prisoners. Each had a different personality which called for different treatment. The meeting with each was the experience of a lifetime. When I came to the cell of Julius Streicher the air of solemnity was gone and in its place was grotesque and vulgar comedy.

The leader of the anti-Semitic sentiment, editor of *Der Stuermer* and famed pornographer, stood, hands on hips in the centre of his cell. He was short and thick-set, wearing only a shirt and trousers. His face was devoid of culture or intellect, lasciviousness and greed showed in every line of his coarse features. Ageing, but physically strong, it was rumoured that he constantly asked the guards for women. When I confronted him, he began to bellow like a bull and flung his arms out in extravagant gestures. His chin was thrust forward in a comic attitude of defiance. He looked at the American interpreter whose appearance was Jewish, and became so agitated that the veins stood out on his primitive forehead. He asked rapid questions in a peculiar snarling voice.

"I want a lawyer who is anti-Semitic. A Jew could not defend *me*. The names on this list look like those of Jews. I am told that some of the judges are Jews."

I listened to this tirade without answer.

Streicher turned on me with a lewd conspiratorial wink.

"The Herr Major is not a Jew. He will help me to find a lawyer."

I could not stop laughing at this foul old creature, past redemption.

"Do you know any lawyers in Nuremberg?"

"Well, I know Dr. Marx. I do not know his address, I am without friends."

"We will make enquiries about Dr. Marx."

I left Streicher's cell in a good humour. I had enjoyed meeting this ridiculous person because of the light which it threw on Hitler's choice of propagandists. If it had not been for the terrible evidence of slaughter and persecution of Jews that lay in the files of the Allied Prosecution I could have thought of Julius Streicher only as a nasty old man.

The boots of our party must have sounded like a firing squad to the prisoners on the ground floor. When we came to Alfried Rosenberg's cell he was trembling. His yellow, bilious face had the expression of a sick spaniel and he preserved a timid silence throughout the proceedings. The chief Jew-baiter had been loud and vocal, but the arch-philosopher of racial theories spoke only a few words in a faltering academic voice. He was, like Streicher, responsible for the crudest form of anti-Semitic propaganda, but there was no trace of the tedious mysticism and obscure philosophies which he used to propound. He had no suggestions to offer for his defence. He knew no lawyers who could represent him.

"I believe that Dr. Frank who is a legal man could assist me. May I be given permission to see him?" He asked this in his trim voice.

"Yes, that can be done," I said.

Again, I could not avoid a smile. The idea of the Butcher of the Eastern territories consulting the Butcher of Poland on the best lawyer to defend him on a charge of mass murder had in it a grim humour. I could still remember those arrogant German farmers with their whips, those young S.S. men marching through the streets of Wlocawek, as Norman Forbes and I, weary and footsore, had given them the Nazi salute on Hitler's birthday. I was no longer there to salute but curiously enough to ensure that these cruel men should receive fair trial according to the best traditions of justice. What a mad world!

Next in this macabre parade, came von Papen attempting an air of old-world courtesty; von Neurath courteous and uninteresting; Dr. Schacht loftily claiming that he expected to be acquitted because he was only a banker, and Albert Speer. Speer had an expressive face in which Nazi ideology and good nature were about equally combined. The real author of the vast slave labour programme for Germany's war production, he disarmed all at Nuremberg with his pleasant smile.

The afternoon wore on until we came at length to the cell of Joachim von Ribbentrop, the Second Bismarck. I was shocked at his appearance. He was bent and ageing. Only a few thin wisps of hair were to be seen above his careworn face. His eyes were deepset and tortured. He retained only a deep and agreeable bass voice.

As I talked of getting counsel for him he began to wring his hands in a piteous fashion and implore me to help him.

"What am I to do? Where can I find a lawyer?"

"Do you know any lawyers?"

"I have never known any lawyers in my life except Dr.

Seapini who is a well-known criminal advocate. I met him once years ago."

"We will try and get him for you."

Ribbentrop's hands were clenched in dismay. I thought that he was about to weep.

There was perhaps no figure in the Nazi hierarchy in whose plight I felt a greater interest. For Ribbentrop with all his vanity and bambast, was a weak and sensitive man. His sense of inferiority led him to exaggerate the "decadence" of England and to persuade the Fuehrer that she would not fight. He would have regarded my early career and education as useless and part of an obsolete system, ripe for Hitler's New Order.

It was with some astonishment that I heard him make application for various aristocratic witnesses from England to attend on his behalf. He said that there were lords and ladies who could give evidence of his desire for peace.

"Send in their names to the General Secretary's Office," I said with impatience.

"You will help me, please, Herr Major"

"I will do what I can."

I turned and left the cell and walked slowly back to the iron grille at the entrance. I felt that I had in a few hours lived the tragedy of a whole generation. A gaoler unlocked the grille and I paused for a moment outside the prison. Deep clouds were threatening the dying sunlight of the October evening, and with Mr. Willey I went to make my report to the Judges of the four Allied powers.

CHAPTER XVI

THE eight Nuremberg judges sat at a long table. Lord Justice Lawrence (now Lord Oaksey) presided and on either side of him were the judges of America, France and the Soviet Union. Microphones for their interpreters had not yet been installed in the room adjoining the court which was used for private sessions of the Tribunal. I rose to make my report on my visits to the prisoners and as I began to speak, the interpreters translated my words in a soft undercurrent.

Between the two Soviet judges a beautiful red-haired Russian girl quietly intoned her version of my speech.

The Soviet judges, General Nikitchenko and Colonel Volchkov alone wore uniform. They sat motionless in their grey tunics with epaulettes and facings of maroon and gold. The pince-nez spectacles of General Nikitchenko reflected the sunlight but, behind them, his eyes seemed cold and inattentive. Colonel Volchkov was writing my name in large Russian characters on a piece of paper.

When I had finished the judges began to discuss whether the prisoners should be allowed to choose former members of the National-Socialist party as their counsel. The Soviet judges swiftly came to life, like animated statues. They attacked the proposal with warmth but they were outvoted by the other judges.

Further measures were discussed for ensuring fair trial for the prisoners. These august men, high representatives of Justice, calmly considered the rights before the law of men accused of the murder of millions. Scoffers and cynics in this impatient age will always contend that the trial should have been summary and short. Yet the Soviet judges, despite their searing hatred of the Germans tried, according to their lights, to understand Western methods and principles.

Handsome, spare, sardonic, Mr. Francis Biddle, former Attorney-General of the United States now spoke, and his words were translated by the interpreters in a chorus of whispering. His colleague, bluff and kindly Judge Parker, followed him. The French Judges, Professor Donnedieu de Vabres and Monsieur Falco quietly made their neat and learned interventions. Then Sir Norman Birkett, with grave eloquence and persuasive clarity, won over his colleagues so that General Nikitchenko nodded in agreement and his eyes smiled faintly behind his pince-nez.

When the discussion was over, Lord Justice Lawrence, dignified and judicial, turned to me.

"The Tribunal is anxious that every facility should be given to the prisoners for their defence. It directs you to continue to procure counsel for them. German counsel will be required for the organisations declared criminal in the indictment: The Corps of Political Leaders of the National-Socialist Party, the Gestapo and S.D., the S.S., the S.A., and the General Staff of the Armed Forces."

I bowed to the Tribunal, picked up my uniform cap and papers and left the room. With Captain Fisher of the U.S. Air Force, one of Mr. Biddle's aides, and a brilliant young lawyer, I walked along the wide stone corridors of the Palace of Justice.

There was twilight in the prison when we came to the cell of Ernst Kaltenbrunner, Chief of the Reich Security Headquarters and second only to Himmler in control of the grim hierarchy of secret police which comprised the Gestapo and S.D.

At that time there were no lights in the cells though they were later installed. When the door opened a dark figure lurked in the shadows. It moved into the centre of the cell so that I could discern a tall, lean man with a long pointed chin. On each of his grey cheeks were duelling scars.

There was an atmosphere of corruption and decay in the cell. This was the successor to Heydrich. He was humbled, and his mind had lost its balance. The tears rolled down his thin face as he wrung his hands in anguish. His great body swayed.

"Kaltenbrunner," I said sharply.

"Yes." From the broken monster came a soft Austrian voice. He choked back his sobs.

"Do you wish the Tribunal to find a lawyer for you?"

"Who would defend me? I have no friends. Please find me a lawyer if you can." His tears caused me no embarrassment.

The door slammed in his face and through the inspection window I could see him lurking once more in the dark corner of the cell, like a sick beast.

Fisher and I left the prison. It had been a strange experience. Kaltenbrunner had personally inspected the methods of 'liquidation' used at Mauthausen concentration camp. In this same camp escaped prisoners of war had been shot on his orders. Under his direction six million men and women had perished as part of the 'final solution' to the Jewish problem. And now he asked to see his family! It was some time before either of us spoke.

"Kaltenbrunner is in tough shape, Major," said Fisher.

"So what!"

"Yeah, so what!"

For nearly a month I saw the prisoners every day. Goering was pleased with his counsel, Dr. Otto Stahmer, a small wizened man from Hamburg. Goering asked frequently for the private interpreter which he was never allowed. Sometimes the fat Reichsmarschall glowed with schoolboy humour, at other times he had moods of black depression. Hess was wayward and childish, regaining for short intervals his lost memory of the past. Von Ribbentrop dismissed his representative Dr. Fritz Sauter of Munich when the trial had been in progress for some weeks. The Tribunal sent me to see him.

He had regained something of his former pretentious-ness. His face had a half-scowling expression.

"I regret to say that Dr. Sauter did not wish me a Happy New Year on the first of January."

Only a year before, this arrogant and stupid man had been the Foreign Minister of Nazi Germany. I could imagine an obsequious Foreign Office Staff lined up to greet him on New Year's Morning.

The Tribunal allowed him another counsel.

As for the wretched Kaltenbrunner, he was found one evening unconscious in his cell. He had suffered a severe cerebral haemorrhage. I saw him in hospital after the trial began, a macabre figure swathed in a blanket. In December he recovered a little and sat with the others in the dock.

When the great trial began on 20th November, 1945 I had been able, with the assistance of military authorities in the four zones of occupation, to find counsel for all the prisoners and for the accused organisations. I had interviewed scores of threadbare German lawyers in the Palace of Justice. Many were reluctant to appear on behalf of the Nazi leaders. Yet in the end a Roman Catholic defended Kalten-brunner, and the absent Martin Bormann, of evil fame, was represented by a lawyer who wrote verse in his leisure hours.

The poetic justice, with which Fate had brought me face to face with my former captors seemed to inspire my next post on the staff of the Tribunal. I was given the high sounding title of "Chief Commissioner for Criminal Organisation," and my task was an enormous one. By now a Lieutenant-Colonel, I sat in a courtroom in the Palace of Justice listening to interminable evidence of the defence of the Gestapo and other groups charged with war crimes and crimes against humanity. Four assistant commissioners were appointed to help me and in a few months over a hundred witnesses were heard and hundreds of thousands of affidavits from Nazi inmates of prison camps examined.

The witnesses for the General Staff and High Command included Field-Marshals von Runstedt, von Manstein, Kesselring and von Brauchitsch. Von Brauchitsch, commander-in-chief of the Army until 1941, who had made a statement to the prosecution, was cross-examined by German counsel for the General Staff.

He sat at a little table in front of my desk, answering questions. He wore a smart field-grey tunic, without badges of rank or decorations, like his fellow Field-Marshals. He had a high bald forehead and his hair was dark at the temples. Only once did he change the tone of his correct Prussian voice. He banged on the table with his fist.

"You do not know what a military genius Hitler was. Only someone who knew him could understand the influence he exercised over others!"

Again he banged on the table so that I became annoyed and told him to be quiet. He rose and bowed apologetically, his black field boots making a faint creaking.

"You must forgive my agitation, Herr Oberst-leutnant."

It was no more than four years since that fine spring morning at Thorn. Sentries and prisoners were cheerful and laughing. The German general seated in his car, adjusted his monocle to look at Forbes and I as we marched to the dentist's hut at the start of our escape. How gay and exciting that morning had been!

Now the world seemed full of sickening hypocrisy. The Field-Marshals who sat before the little table in the courtroom denied that there had been a general staff and High Command. There was only Adolf Hitler. According to these aristocrats of a military caste, Corporal Hitler was not the madman they had supposed but a soldier of genius. When the witnesses for the Gestapo and S.S. declared ignorance of Himmler's vast apparatus of torture, I began to wonder if the Gestapo building at Plock had ever existed except in my nightmares.

A year passed and autumn leaves began to fall again in the courtyard of Nuremberg prison. Often I saw the prisoners take their exercise, walking in a circle like the inmates of the town gaol at Colditz. The day came for them to receive sentence and I watched them go down from the dock for the last time. Already the world, hungry for new sensations, had begun to forget them. Goering, Ribbentrop and Streicher were fast becoming figures of legend. They seemed no longer living symbols of terror and persecution.

Racked by disease and madness, they were led out to die like captured beasts of prey. Keitel stood to attention in the dock. He had been allowed to change his carpet slippers for his fieldboots. Lord Justice Lawrence, without the scarlet robes and black cap of a Judge of Assize, in a quiet even voice sentenced him to death. Keitel winced at the disgrace of hanging. He clicked his heels and bowed.

*　　　*　　　*

I had seen the twelvemonth tragedy played in full and known intimately the actors on the stage. I had seen Goering wilt and grow pale under the lash of Sir David Maxwell-Fyfe. I had escaped from the darkness as a mere lieutenant to sit in judgment on field-marshals and leaders of the German State. These were my thoughts as the Dakota which flew me to England rose over Nuremberg. The ruins, bathed in red sunset, glowed like a funeral pyre. What lay further on the road that led from the wicket-gate in the moat-bridge?

Ten years have passed since I escaped from Colditz; much has happened to me since Pat Reid picked the lock of the door of the attic above the guard-house and released Luteyn and me into the world. For the next five years, after my return home, I was actively engaged in the study of escape as a science.

Like the escapers of the first world war, Forbes and I and many others of our contemporaries were pioneers; the lessons we learned will be elementary knowledge to future prisoners of war. But this knowledge will be insufficient without the gay and determined spirit that inspired us in the early months of the last war.

It was not long after my return from Nuremberg that my professional duties as a barrister brought me again within prison walls. Even now, years afterwards, when I visit cells beneath the courts where counsel interview their clients I am affected by the stale smell of food eaten in a narrow space, and again I am aware of that feeling of life apart from the world which I experienced for twenty long months.

When I look round these cells, I think again of those days in the town gaol of Colditz. The prisoner of war is not a criminal, yet he must employ all the criminal's ingenuity and cunning. The criminal picks locks and uses all his other artifices for anti-social purposes and material gain. Many of them enjoy prison because of its modern amenities, so they have not the same incentive to escape as the prisoner of war.

The road from Nuremberg also led me into politics, and politics led me first to the dock gates, where my audience received me without enthusiasm. They voted overwhelmingly for my opponent. My next Parliamentary election in 1951 was the high spot of many ironical situations. My opponent on this occasion was a pacifist and a temperance reformer, and he beat me by 120 votes in a poll of 53,000!

How Hauptmann Priem would have laughed! But he lost his opportunity, because Schnapps took him off before the war ended.

P. R. Reid M.B.E., M.C.

The Colditz Story

Colditz—the German POW camp that was infamous in its captors and famous for its captives.

Here is the world-famous story that has now passed into legend, the story of the incredible courage and dare-devil ingenuity of those who burrowed and leaped, fought and ran their way to freedom.

The story of the finest escapers of World War II, culminating in the author's own dramatic escape in 1942.

NOW A THRILLING T.V. SERIAL

The Latter Days at Colditz

Here is the thrilling sequel to THE COLDITZ STORY.

Here are all the courage and bravado, daring and skill that made THE COLDITZ STORY into an international bestseller.

Here are the German bullies and the indestructible prisoners of war, the gruelling conditions and the almost nonchalant brutality that went to make Oflag VIIC the most feared and hated hell-hole that any captive could fear to see.

And here again is a story of brave and red-blooded action, of the sort of heroism that makes gods of mere men.

THE CORONET WAR LIBRARY

All these books are available at your bookshop or newsagent, or can be ordered direct from the publisher. Just tick the titles you want and fill in the form below.

CORONET BOOKS, Cash Sales Department, Kernick Industrial Estate, Penryn, Cornwall.

Please send cheque or postal order. No currency, and allow 7p per book (6p per book on orders of five copies and over) to cover the cost of postage and packing in U.K., 7p per copy overseas.

Name ....

Address...